KAELA SANER

I Trust You, Lord

Letters to God on Psalm 31

Contents

Introduction

I was seventeen years old when I decided to surrender my life to God. It was a life-changing, transformative decision that has had its twist and turns. Before that, I'd never known there was a God. I'd heard about Him but never gone to church and never grown up in a household that honored God. It was through my parent's divorce that my eyes were opened. Open to the discovery of God. Open to the True God. Open to surrendering to God.

Most people seem to think that once you surrender your life to God, it is a cakewalk. But that is far from true. Surrendering your life to God is the hardest walk that you will take. The walk of being a true Christian can't mean just giving God a portion of your heart and then walking in the ways of the world. No. Being a true Christian requires sacrifice. Surrendering your whole mind, body, heart, and soul. Being a Christian is endurance, patience, and perseverance.

When I surrendered my life to God, I didn't understand that. Nobody told me how hard it would be. I had no comprehension of anything regarding God. To understand Him and His ways, I had to walk up a big mountain. I had to become humbled before the throne. My journey resulted in a lot of heartbreak coupled with unspeakable joy. Most importantly, my eyes and ears became open to the ways of God, to the Holy Spirit. My heart burst with the love, forgiveness, and protection of God. I had to learn and understand God's ways. I am still constantly learning His ways and the goodness of Himself.

Every single time I read the Bible, I always find something new or a revelation for a situation. I love to study it and to know more about who God is and who Jesus is. It was there where I discovered my two favorite books. The first, the book of Hebrews that describes who Jesus is, what He did for us, and the testimonies of faith. My second favorite book is the book of Psalms. We are going to focus on the book of Psalms. Don't get me wrong, I love every one of the books of the Bible, but Psalms connects me in a special way to who my God is. It shows me the heart of God. Why would it not? Psalms was written by David, a man after God's own heart. I aspire to be just like David and Jesus—a *woman* after God's own heart.

I've chosen to center this book on the book of Psalms because it includes many songs of praise, spiritual praise. They offer worship and glory to the Most High with words full of wisdom and significance. Psalms is no easy book to digest. It includes reprimands of sinners and righteous vengeance against idolatry. Yet at the core is the love of God and forgiveness for the ungodly. He is lifted and praised for His glory, for who He is. For what He does for His children. Psalms is a book that is centered on the heart of the believer. That they belong to God. Evermore, the book of Psalms is a declaration that there is only one true God, Jehovah.

Specifically, I have focused my reflections here on Psalm 31, which traverses from who God is to God's vengeance on idols to whose we are. It shows a wide range of the character of God. Psalm 31 is a lament psalm written by David when he was going through a trying time in his life. A lament is when a person prays or cries out to God in anguish during their trial. David brings comfort to all who read Psalm 31 that God will never leave them or forsake them. That God is always a present savior and a present help. This psalm brings me closer to God because it gives me confidence during my trials. It brings me an expectancy that my God will deliver me and bring me victory in my trials.

I've written in the format of letters directed to God from one of his children. They are written by me, obviously, but I encourage you, the reader, to make them your own, to take up the role of letter-writer. Maybe you will find that they express exactly what you wanted to say, or maybe you have something a bit different to say. That's okay. They're intended to share my own experience of God and of my life with Him, as well as to encourage you to pour all your heart and soul out to Him. Read them with an honest, open heart and a bare soul.

Note: All Scripture passages in this book are taken from the King James Version.

Letter 1

My Righteous Jehovah

"In thee, O LORD, do I put my trust; let me never be ashamed: deliver me in thy righteousness."
Psalm 31:1

Dear God,

In You alone I trust. I place my trust in You, I believe in You. As I have come to learn, the Hebrew word for "trust" according to Strong's Concordance is *chacah*, meaning "to flee for protection, to confide in, often used where God is compared to a rock or a shield or one with protective wings." Trust in You is critical to my faith, critical to knowing You and knowing Your character. It *is* Your character. Faith. As Timothy says, "If we believe not, *yet* he abideth faithful: he cannot deny himself" (2 Tim. 2:13). I write this letter to You, God, for everyone who needs to know *whose* they are. They need to know the trust and faithfulness of You. They need to trust in Your unfailing faith.

Trust is faith. Without trust in You, I have no faith. No faith that You will bring me through the hills and valleys, no faith that You will do what You have promised You will do. No faith that You, my God are my Father, my friend, my shield, my rock, and my protector. But I *must* have trust and faith in Jehovah. How could I not? Are You not my God who brought me through my darkness? Provided for me? Rescued me from my destruction? Are You not my God who loves me so much that You gave Your one and only Son to be sacrificed on the cross for me? Yes, You are Lord! For You are *Jehovah Eli*, the Lord my God!

You are the One whom I go to for protection. You provide me with the belt of truth, the shield of faith, the breastplate of righteousness, the shoes of peace, and the sword of the Spirit, the Word (Eph. 6:13-17). You are the One I confide all my secrets to, because You already know everything about me. You know all my secrets, all my darkness, all my vulnerabilities, and all the things I cry about. I need to confide in You to lift the invisible weight. My God who knows all is ever there, ever faithful, my Comforter. Surely You cover me underneath Your wings as my Protector. As the Scriptures say, "But they that wait upon the Lord shall renew *their* strength; they shall mount up with wings as eagles; they shall run, and not be weary; *and* they shall walk, and not faint" (Isa. 40:31). You are my lamp upon my feet, and, Lord, You will always hold my right hand. Forgive me for losing my trust and faith in You. For I *must* trust You, Abba, with all my heart and soul. You already have faith in me. Now it is my turn to have faith in You.

Hebrews 11 is the Hall of Fame of Faith. There are scores of Your people who demonstrated great acts of faith in You. Your people come in all shapes and sizes. They range from Abraham to Jesus to Paul, so many people that Your faithful writer could not name all of them. It is amazing all You can accomplish in us, whether our faith is little or great. These people show me that "faith is an unshakable and unbreakable belief that will do everything He has promised to do even before there is visible evidence to that effect."[1] Your people were bold in their faith in You, Jehovah. They knew that You were always for them and never against them, that through their faith in You, You would always deliver.

As the Apostle Paul wrote, "But without faith *it is* impossible to please *him*: for he that cometh to God must believe that he is, and that he is a rewarder of them that diligently seek him" (Heb. 11:6).

Lord, their faith in You never shamed them because of their undying devotion. All they ever saw was You. So often I see Your people being ridiculed for whom they place their faith in, bringing a sense of shame upon their hearts. The word You have placed upon my heart now is *ashamed*. In Hebrew it is *buwsh*, meaning to feel worthless. Lord, no one should ever feel worthless in Your eyes, and I know You never see anyone as worthless. Not even the most egregious sinner is worthless in Your eyes. Truthfully, it is only Your eyes that matter. It is by my faith that my worthlessness turns into righteousness. Even if I have just a mustard seed of faith, my worthlessness gets cleansed along with my sins. My brother Jesus is the One who has cleansed and washed my worthlessness away! He is the One who died for me, and He is the One who did not feel ashamed for His death. No, my God, he died for me so that I could be cleansed of my sins, washed anew, and be in union with Him. To trust in Jesus is to know He will never put me to shame.

Abba, to trust in Your righteousness delivers me from my worthlessness. You will deliver me in my worthlessness by the faith I have in Your righteousness. A righteousness that is received only by my faith in You. Thus, "Faith is the means by which a person is justified and the action through which a person receives the righteousness of Christ."[2] Yes, Abba, You will deliver me in Your righteousness because of my faith in Jesus and my trust in You! As Your Word says,

> Even the righteousness of God *which* is by faith of Jesus Christ unto all and upon all them that believe: for there is no difference: For all have sinned, and come short of the glory of God; Being justified freely by his grace through the redemption that is in Christ Jesus: Whom God hath set forth

to be a propitiation through faith in his blood, to declare his righteousness for the remission of sins that are past, through the forbearance of God; To declare, I *say*, at this time his righteousness: that he might be just, and justifier of him which believeth in Jesus. (Rom. 3:22-26)

Your Son sacrificed Himself voluntarily for me. For the world. The shedding of His blood cleanses me of my sins and unites me with You, but it was also an act of mercy for Your people. God, You could have easily unleashed Your wrath and punishment. Instead, You sent Your one and only Son to be sacrificed. He established His righteousness for me because He is just.

You have given me the insight that righteousness is a relationship between You and Your child that is bonded with faith. For You are always faithful, but, God, *my* faith does waiver. It does crumble when unforeseen circumstances come into my life. Yet I know that my faith will not be destroyed, because You are God, Jehovah. The lifter of my head, the promise keeper, the deliverer, and the righteous.

In the story of Moses, I see how You called him to deliver Your people from bondage into the Promised Land. Moses did not believe he could be Your chosen. Moses's unbelief ranged from thinking he was not the right person for Your will to objecting because of his stuttering speech to questioning You about what he should tell Your people. Even after he had spoken all his fears and problems to You, You still chose him. He chose to serve You. He accepted Your invitation of righteousness and that acceptance led to the promise of deliverance.

And God spake unto Moses, and said unto him, I *am* the LORD: And I appeared unto Abraham, unto Isaac, and unto Jacob, by *the name* of God Almighty, but by my name JEHOVAH was I not known to them. And I have also established my covenant with them, to give them the land of Canaan, the land of their pilgrimage, wherein they were strangers. And I have also heard the groaning of the children of Israel, whom the Egyptians keep in bondage; and I have remembered my covenant. Wherefore say unto the children of Israel, *I am* the LORD, and I will bring you out from under the burdens of the Egyptians, and I will rid you out of their bondage, and I will redeem you with a stretched out arm, and with great judgements: And I will take you to me for a people, and I will be to you a God: and ye shall know that *I am* the LORD your God, which bringeth you out from under the burdens of the Egyptians. And I will bring you in unto the land, concerning the which I did swear to give it to Abraham, to Isaac, and to Jacob; and I will give it you for an heritage: *I am* the LORD. (Exod. 6:2-8)

To have unshakable, unbreakable faith like Moses is to know without a shadow of a doubt that You, God, are the promiser of deliverance and righteousness.

Faith is a way of life. Your way of life. It is trusting in You to deliver me in Your righteousness. For I live by faith, by believing rather than by seeing (2 Cor. 5:7). That belief delivers me unto Jesus, declaring that He lives in me (Gal. 2:20) and knowing it is Him who delivers me in His righteousness.

Your Righteous Servant

Letter 2

The Lord My Defense

*"Bow down thine ear to me; deliver me speedily: be thou my strong rock, for
an house of defence to save me."*
Psalm 31:2

Dear Lord,

You hear, You bow down, and Your ear always hears my cries. To bow
down has a few definitions and one of them is to hear and have a private
conversation with someone, but that person doesn't necessarily have to
listen or hear. However, God, You do bow down Your ear to hear my
cries. But what is amazing is You also speak to me. You do listen and
hear me! I hear that small voice that is undeniably You flowing with the
Holy Spirit. The power, love, and all-knowingness behind that small
voice is all I need to know that it *is* You, God.

There is no denying that You do speak to Your people. In Hebrew, "to
bow down" is *natah*. Strong's Concordance defines *natah* as "to stretch
forth, to spread out, stretch down, turn aside." Lord, You stretch forth
and down to hear my cries and to speak Your truth into my ears. Truly,
Abba, You do not need to stretch forth and down to hear me because

You are God. You already know my thoughts before I even say them. Rather, You hear Your people out of love. You want to hear my cries, to hear my pleas that You are the only One I need. And there is the start of something new, the start of You receiving all the glory. For "I waited patiently for the LORD; and he inclined unto me, and heard my cry" (Ps. 40:1).

Interestingly, Lord, You have designed us so that the ear, heart, and mind are in tandem. Proverbs says, "So that thou incline thine ear unto wisdom, *and* apply thine heart to understanding" (2:2). Yes, Abba, when You hear me my heart and mind take notice. Lord, I know You incline Your ear toward me, indicating that You are indeed willing to hear what needs to be told. For though You are God, You also love Your people so much that You will hear them. I give thanks to You, Abba, for hearing Your people and showing grace! Lord, the Scriptures say, "In my distress I called upon the LORD, and cried to my God: and he did hear my voice out of his temple, and my cry *did enter* into his ears" (2 Sam. 22:7). You entreat me to heed Your Voice, and so I *must* heed Your Voice. I *must* incline my ear to You. It is imperative of me, because though You will hear me, I *must* obey Your commands, for You are my God.

When I do not listen and obey You, Lord, my heart and mind become more susceptible to the world. Instead of using me for Your purposes You choose someone else who will listen and obey Your Voice. My refusal to hear You becomes the unmistakable, dreadful sin. The sin of disobedience. Oh, what great sorrow weighs me down. Forgive me, God, for not hearing You.

> Behold, the LORD's hand is not shortened, that it cannot save; neither his ear heavy, that it cannot hear: But your iniquities have separated between you and your God, and your sins have hid *his* face from you, that he will not hear. (Isa. 59:1-2)

Though inevitably, I stumble through this tragedy, my God, You always provide a way for me. Thank you, God, for delivering a way to remedy the unimaginable. Lord, Your antidote is Jesus. He is the way, the truth, the life (see John 14:6).

I must repent of my sins, for Jesus died for me to be cleansed and to be in unity with Him. "Now we know that God heareth not sinners: but if any man be a worshipper of God, and doeth his will, him he heareth" (John 9:31). O God, I know You do not want my ears closed off; You want them open to hear Your still, small voice. You want me to hear Your holiness, love, and forgiveness. To listen to and obey Your commands that are always for me, never against me. God, I need Your Voice. It sustains me! You are a mighty God who does not loathe anyone, for we are all Your children. Mighty in strength and wisdom.

Surely, Lord, You do not let the wicked thrive, because You are a just God to the stricken. Never will You take Your eyes off those who obey and listen to Your commands. For the chains that bind the wicked holds them in affliction. You show them who their God is. On display are the sins of their prideful nature, their selfishness. Abba, their ears have to be open to Your discipline and Your commands for them to turn from their iniquities (see Job 36:5-10). I petition on their behalf for You to have mercy upon them. Open their ears, hearts, and mind, as You have done for me! Turn their ears upon the Good Shepherd. Jesus tells the Pharisees, "To him the porter openeth; and the sheep hear his voice: and he calleth his own sheep by name, and leadeth them out" (John 10:3).

You do more than just listen and bow Your ear. Action takes place when You hear my distress. You rescue me because You are my strong rock. You are the God who listens to the pleas and cries, the tears of my prayers. When my heart is overwhelmed, You will lead me to the rock of Your safety, becoming a strong tower and a shelter from the enemy. Abba, with much fervency I declare that You are my sanctuary! Safe am

I beneath the shelter of Your wings (see Ps. 61:1-4).

It is no accident that Your beloved David, the psalmist, describes You as a strong rock. For "a rock provides a solid foundation, protection, and security."[3] David praised You when You rescued him from all his enemies. David described You, Abba, as a rock, a fortress, a savior, and a protector.

> And he said, the LORD *is* my rock, and my fortress, and my deliverer; The God of my rock; in him will I trust: *he is* my shield, and the horn of my salvation, my high tower, and my refuge, my saviour; thou savest me from violence. I will call on the LORD, who is worthy to be praised: so shall I be saved from mine enemies. (2 Sam. 22: 2-4)

Lord, You are no ordinary rock; You are *the* rock who sustains. You are the mighty One who fights my battles and wars.

> How should one chase a thousand, and two put ten thousand to flight, except their Rock had sold them, and the LORD shut them up? For their rock is not as our Rock, even our enemies themselves *being* judges. (Deut. 32:30-31)

Oh yes, You are my Rock, and you have no comparison against my enemies. For You have no equal; You have no rival. My Rock, You speak to me, walk with me, and love me.

My Rock is a firm house of defense. More, You are my *home.* A saving fortress. Wherever You are, Lord, I am. For Your home is my home. It is a place that I worship You. A sanctuary that is full of love, compassion, joy, and laughter. It is a place for rest where I can dwell in Your presence, basking in Your light. Giving You all the praise, glory, and worship that only You deserve. In Your home, peace dwells. The home's foundation is laid with Your peace. When I need Your defense, I run to Your home. For Your home is a house of defense.

Among my enemies, I will know peace, because I am surrounded by Your home. Your appointed king, David, best described dwelling in Your home:

> One *thing* I have desired of the LORD, that will I seek after; that I may dwell in the house of the LORD all the days of my life, to behold the beauty of the LORD, and to inquire in his temple. For in the time of trouble he shall hide me in his pavilion: in the secret of his tabernacle shall he hide me; he shall set me up upon a rock. And now shall mine head be lifted up above mine enemies round about me: therefore will I offer in his tabernacle sacrifices of joy; I will sing, yea, I will sing praises unto the LORD. (Ps. 27:4-6)

Your Protected Servant

Letter 3

The Compass of My Feet

"For thou art my rock and my fortress; therefore for thy name's sake lead me, and guide me."
Psalm 31:3

Dear Rock,

You are a rock of refuge. A refuge of You is a safe place of protection, a place for resting and a place for connecting with You. God, You are the refuge and fortress, a fortress that cannot be penetrated. Like Your people during their journey toward the Promised Land, You

create upon every dwelling place of mount Zion, and upon her assemblies, a cloud and smoke by day, and the shining of a flaming fire by night: for upon all the glory *shall be* a defence. And there shall be a tabernacle for a shadow in the day time from the heat, and for a place of refuge, and for a covert from storm and from rain. (Isa. 4:5-6)

God, You protect me from all the storms! Even from the ones that I have caused, You still protect me! You, Lord, become my Compass, my Rock in the storms. When I can't see beyond my next step, You are always directing and guiding my feet on Your paths.

Lord, forgive me when I become sidetracked. This world, a world ruled by sin, can become my distraction. I will always need You to pull me back with Your Compass. When I am oppressed by the enemy and the things of this world, You become my refuge in times of trouble (see Ps. 9:9). You command me to make You my refuge in which I could never disobey You. You sustain me so that no evil shall befall me and no plague shall come near my home (see Ps. 91:9-10). Jehovah, You always come first as my refuge, not fear. As Your people had to learn and so do I, You instantly become my dwelling when I surrender wholly to You. A dwelling of refuge are You and Your Promised Land waits for those who choose You. It is a Promised Land that is rich in milk, honey, and oil with the overflowing blessings of You.

Time and time again, Lord, You call upon Your people to keep their focus on You. Eyes that are trained on You cross the boundary of the eternal. But those that turn their eyes away become shackled to the enemy. They become chained again. Therefore, I *must* keep my focus on You through all the darkness that surrounds me. I *must* focus on the Compass. I *must* keep my spiritual eyes and ears upon You. For You have put Your light upon me and within me. Abba, You light up my path always. Leading me and guiding me to You, bringing You all the praise, glory, and worship. You see it is You who guides, You who sustains, and You who protects me along the journey. I cannot do it on my own. I will surely fail.

Lord, Your people need to lift their eyes and keep them trained upon You, because peace will blanket them amid the darkness. Turn their eyes upon eternity. It will be peace that comes from Your grace and mercy. For Your grace is sufficient in our weaknesses, and Your mercy is active from the blood of Jesus Christ. You give light to those who sit in darkness. A light that can conquer any darkness. Praise God! Hallelujah! For You guide the feet out of the shadow of death unto the path of peace, the Prince of Peace (see Luke 1:78-79; Isa. 9:6)!

Yet even after I know that You are my Compass, my faith still waivers. The thought that my God will not pull me out of the darkness, that You will not guide me, not protect me, and not deliver me, floats through the mind. Lord, I seem to only torture myself with those egregious thoughts. Please open my eyes and ears! You are the foundation of my guidance, renewing my strength, guiding me on the right path, thus bringing You all the glory and praise You more than deserve.

By the Holy Spirit will the path be revealed and the truth of guidance be heard. "Howbeit when he, the Spirit of truth, is come, he will guide you into all truth: for he shall not speak of himself; but whatsoever he shall hear, *that* shall he speak: and he will shew you things to come" (John 16:13). The truth of guidance *will be* heard, but only with ears, eyes, and heart open by humility, truthfulness, and discernment. Humble me, my God! Humble my prideful and selfish heart! You will guide those who are humble in Your just ways, and You will teach the humility of Your ways (see Ps. 25:9).

For Your ways are always perfect. Your ways are always higher than my ways. I have to be truthful and honest with myself. If I am dishonest, the Compass will become my misdirection (see Prov. 11:3). Lord, sometimes my honesty needs Your direction, needs Your discernment of the truth. Discernment is Your wisdom. The prophet Hosea made this known, "Who is wise, and he shall understand these *things*? prudent, and he shall know them? for the ways of the LORD *are* right, and the just shall walk in them: but the transgressors shall fall therein" (Hosea 14:9). Without Your discernment, I am just walking without Your Compass. I am walking blindly. Lord, cover my eyes with mud to open them to Your wonderful world! Place in my heart the Compass of Your Heart!

16

Your Misdirected Child

Letter 4

My Deliverer and My Strength

"Pull me out of the net that they have laid privily for me: for thou art my strength."
Psalm 31:4

Dear God,

You are my deliverer, the deliverer from my enemies and the trap of the wickedness. Furthermore, "a trap is used to show the dominion of the one who casts the net or sets it, accompanied by the powerlessness of the one who is caught in it."[4] The trap my enemies lay for me gives me two choices: to be captured or to look to the One who is my Deliverer. The choice is simple; there is no deceit in my answer. There is no mistaking that my enemies are consumed by darkness. The enemies of the Lord are enemies of mine. They are consumed by a darkness that I cannot trust. They are captured by the wicked trap of the true enemy, Satan. Indeed, they are wily with an insatiable appetite to kill, steal, and destroy. When I am faced with such dire circumstances, such dire enemies, I ask myself who I will I look to. Fear? Anxiety? Hopelessness?

No, I surely cannot look at my enemies. I am not a reflection of my enemies' eyes. When I look in the mirror, I see all the things and blessings You have done for me, Lord, and I dare say I will most certainly not cave to the insecurities within me! God, You are always guiding me on Your paths, and when I walk through the valley of the shadow of death, I will fear no evil. For You are my rod and staff, my Comforter (see Ps. 23:3-4). I *will* certainly look to You, God, who has never failed me nor forsaken me! I *will* look to You who saves me and loves me unfailingly! I *will* look to my God who forgives me of all transgressions! I *will* look to You who is my warrior and my Deliverer!

I admit, Abba, that sometimes I do stumble and fall. Sometimes I will not see the trap coming. My focus becomes diverted from You. I become focused on myself. I do become blinded by the ways of the enemy because my focus is on this world. My focus is on man. Steady my eyes on Your eternity. Stay my eyes on the One who created me. Show me what no fear is, for You are always walking beside me. I could not see You before, because my eyes were trained on the distractions. When I become trained on You, Lord, peace will consume me, and my enemies will be the ones to stumble and fall. The enemy will be squashed beneath my heel, and I will grab hold of the victory that I already had. Yes, God, You are my warrior, You are *Jehovah Nissi* (the Lord my Banner). Your Word says,

> The LORD is my light and my salvation; whom shall I fear? The LORD is the strength of my life; of whom shall I be afraid? When the wicked, *even* mine enemies and my foes, came upon me to eat up my flesh, they stumbled and fell. Though an host should encamp against me, my heart shall not fear: though war should rise against me, in this *will* I *be* confident. (Ps. 27:1-3)

In my many trials, Lord, You have shown me that You are a just God and

You promise a just punishment for my enemies. Oh yes, my enemies *are* conquered. God, You do not let the wicked live in Your eternity. Instead, You give justice to those who are distressed (see Job 36:6). As You spoke to Isaiah,

> For I the LORD love judgement, I hate robbery for burnt offering; and I will direct their work in truth, and I will make an everlasting covenant with them. And their seed shall be known among the Gentiles, and their offspring among the people: all that see them shall acknowledge them, that they *are* the seed *which* the LORD hath blessed. (Isa. 61: 8-9)

Inside the wickedness, the trap has failed. From the inside out, the wicked are corrupt and defile anything they touch. Yes, the wickedness failed because of their own black hearts, black hearts that turned on them. Lord, You saved me from the evilness of their ways. You delivered me from the trap of wickedness. Once I was conquered, now I conquer them.

You are ever the Deliverer; more, You are the Strength. My strength. When I have Your strength, it is my defense. No one or nothing can break through that defense because it is a spiritual strength gifted by Your grace. God, You have given me the free will to make my own decision. Thus, I can reject the gift due to my unbelief. I cannot be strong on my own. My strength only relies upon the principles of this world, the principles of self that say "I can do this, I did all the hard work, by my strength was I able to accomplish this or that." But Your strength is eternal. Your strength has been here since the start of creation, flowing through past, present, and future, bringing deliverance to all Your people and judgment upon Your enemies.

From the moment You created this world, You showed Your ultimate strength. You created all the stars and gave each one a name, not missing

a single one. Your mighty strength has no equal or rival (see Isa. 40:26).
Yes, from the start of creation, You knew there would only be One who
could ever have Your ultimate strength, only One who could ever be
one hundred percent human and one hundred percent God, only One
who brought deliverance to Your people. That One is Jesus.

> Behold, the Lord GOD will come with strong *hand*, and his
> arm shall rule for him: behold, his reward *is* with him, and
> his work before him. He shall feed his flock like a shepherd:
> he shall gather the lambs with his arm, and carry *them* in his
> bosom, *and* shall gently lead those that are with young. (Isa.
> 40:10-11)

I look to Jesus for my strength, the One who sacrificed everything and
died a criminal's death. He was beaten, whipped, bruised, and crushed
but kept going, finishing the race. He did not stop until He rose three
days later. With a heart that aches for Him but also with a heart full of
understanding, I know that He *is* strength. The strength is given to Him
by You, Father, a strength that brought glory to You, expressing Your
character and sustaining everything by the Word of Your power. At
Your right hand He sits because of His mighty strength (see Heb. 1:3).

My strength is found only in You. Even in my weaknesses, I can only
find Your strength. Your Word comforts me for I know,

> The LORD *is* my strength and my shield; my heart trusted in
> him, and I am helped: therefore my heart greatly rejoiceth;
> and with my song I will praise him. The LORD *is* their
> strength, and he *is* the saving strength of his anointed. (Ps.
> 28:7-8)

I know I can do anything through Christ who gives me strength (see

Phil. 4:13). I know that even when I am lacking strength You restore me. You restore my heart and soul to Your strength. Faith as small as a mustard seed is I all I need to receive Your restoration. For You give power to the weak and strength to the powerless (see Isa. 40:29). What brings even greater joy and laughter is knowing that Your grace is *sufficient*. "My grace is sufficient for thee: for my strength is made perfect in weakness" (2 Cor. 12:9). What a powerful and mighty God I have!

Your Restored Servant

Letter 5

My Redeemer, I Trust You

"Into thine hand I commit my spirit, thou hast redeemed me, O LORD God
of truth."
Psalm 31:5

Dear Papa,

Your Word, Psalm 31:5, is a prophetic verse that Your beloved David wrote. It prophesies about Jesus and His sacrifice for us, describing all we need in our redemption. Surrendering all. In the palm of Your hand, I trust You with my spirit. Trust is ever-present. I know it is as You hold me in the palm of Your hands. Because You are truth, therefore, Your trust is planted within my spirit. Though at times, I may become an archeologist looking for the ever-present trust, I know it is always there. I know because Your Holy Spirit constantly reveals it to me. Forgive me for not trusting in you. Forgive me for not surrendering all. I know it is the essence of You; You are always faithful.

Papa, the word for "spirit" in Strong's Concordance is *ruwach*, meaning "breath, air, strength, wind, breeze, spirit, courage, temper, Spirit." There is no denying who the Spirit is. It is my God, the Holy

Spirit. There is no denying whose Spirit I belong to. You are the breath of life flowing through me and empowering me to act in accordance with Your will. Your Spirit is constantly coursing through me, revealing all Your hidden secrets, revealing and convicting all the darkness within me, for I am your Child. With Your hands, like a potter, You molded me.

For Your Spirit to course through me, I must surrender all and *trust* You with every fiber within me. I need to trust in all the ashes (my faults) and all the beauty. Frankly, to trust in You, Lord, is an act of abandonment, abandonment of myself and my worldly thinking. My outer self must die for You to breathe life back into my inner self. I need Your *ruwach*!

What astounds me Lord, is that Your *ruwach* became Jesus. He became the *ruwach* when He was crucified. His worldly body died, but His Spirit lives on for eternity. "And when Jesus had cried with a loud voice, he said, Father, into thy hands I commend my spirit: and having said thus, he gave up the ghost" (Luke 23:46). Papa, when Jesus died for me, You redeemed me. Therefore, Jesus paid the ultimate price, releasing me from the power of sin and *empowering* me to redemption.

Lord, You are my redeemer. You are *the* Redeemer, representing completeness, sovereignty, and freedom. My surrender to You ushers in the characteristics of who You are, implanting them on my heart. Lord, I must surrender my heart into Your hands. It is not only my mind that must be complicit; my whole heart and soul must be willing. Papa, give me a willing heart, soul, and spirit, sensitive only to You. I cannot have fear within my heart. I must be willing to release that fear before I can place my heart, soul, and spirit in Your hands. How great You are Lord!

Even before Jesus was crucified and even before He was born, still, Papa, You were redeeming Your people. You love all Your people so much! When You were leading Your people out of Egypt, You did more than just break their bondages. You redeemed Your people from slavery! As David's prayer of thanks proclaims,

> Wherefore thou art great, O LORD God: for *there* is none like thee, neither is *there any* God beside thee, according to all that we have heard with our ears. And what one nation in the earth is like thy people, *even* like Israel, whom God went to redeem for a people to himself, and to make him a name, and to do for you great things and terrible, for thy land, before thy people, which thou redeemedst to thee from Egypt, *from* the nations and their gods? For thou hast confirmed to thyself thy people Israel *to be* a people unto thee forever: and thou, LORD, art become their God. (2 Sam. 7:22-24)

Redeeming Your people is a glimpse of all You can do. You want more from Your children. I need to give You more. You want all to know that You are the One who has redeemed. It was not someone else or a vain god but You, Lord, who has redeemed. You get all the praise, glory, and worship!

As Your people, we must let our old selves be crucified and walk out of the tomb with our new selves, clothed in redemption. The question I ask myself is, how can I do that? It seems rather difficult. But then I wouldn't be honest with You, with myself. I truly have not been listening. Your Son Jesus Christ is the complete and perfect example. He died on that cross as a man shedding His old self and bringing redemption for *all*. Then He rose three days later. Walking out of the tomb in His new self, walking out as Lord, clothed in glory and reverence. Yes! You rescued me from the darkness and brought me to the kingdom of light, in which I have redemption by the blood of Jesus Christ (see Col. 1:13-14). My liberation is possible. It is in my hands! That's the key, though: to choose liberation or to choose shackles. You give me free will to make a choice, and I choose to accept my redemption. I choose Jesus. The Scripture that You have placed within my heart is: "And grieve not the holy Spirit of God, whereby ye are sealed unto the day of redemption" (Eph. 4:30).

The Redeemer You are, but God of Truth is Your name. You are the One who brings truth to my heart and soul. You are a faithful God who is trustworthy. You speak the truth, and Your truths are rooted in Your promises, covenants, and deliverances. A word of truthfulness, You are love by Your faith and Your forgiveness. Everything that is of You is united with Your faithfulness and trustworthiness. For Your Word says, "Thy righteousness *is* an everlasting righteousness and thy law *is* the truth" (Ps. 119:142). You hide nothing from me; it is I who hides everything. Always You want us, Your children, to need You, to want You, to become closer to You, to be of You and not of ourselves. I hide my secrets because my faith waivers and I become distraught. I hide them because I never want to disappoint You. I turn my eyes to the temporary solution. I turn my eyes on myself and eventually turn my back on You who saved me. How selfish I am. Forgive me, O God!

Slowly my faith dwindles, eventually becoming an empty well. Truly I had never considered that I should look at what causes my faith to waiver. I had become so focused on the problem that I never considered looking first toward You and all Your promises. So I hid my secrets, my hurts, and looked toward the worldly solutions that could never fulfill me. My lack of faith caused me to briefly walk off the path, letting the enemy dictate my steps instead of You. My lack of faith caused a feeling of worthlessness to creep in, and I became hypersensitive to only myself. During all the chaos, I had forgotten that I only need faith the size of a mustard seed to move a mountain. If just a small amount of faith can do that to a mountain, what will happen when I have greater faith than a mustard seed?

Your faithfulness never waivers. You are always walking beside me, holding my right hand. The Holy Spirit is there, speaking words of wisdom, truth, and faith. The Holy Spirit is always truthful. Jesus explains to us, "*Even* the Spirit of truth; whom the world cannot receive, because it seeth him not, neither knoweth him: but ye know him; for he dwelleth with you, and shall be in you" (John 14:17). Jesus is always there guiding me along the way, showing me that it is You whom I should look toward, calling me to lift my eyes upon You. For Jesus says, "I am the way, the truth, and the life: no man cometh unto the Father, but by me" (John 14:6). Still, at times when I do not hear or see You, Your Word is there, ever-present, alive, and always truthful. Always comforting. Your Holy Spirit is there within the Word. Your Word says, "Sanctify them through thy truth: thy word is truth" (John 17:17). Yes, God of Truth, You are always there, never giving up on me even when I give up on You.

Your Redeemed Servant

Letter 6

Foolishness

"I have hated them that regard lying vanities: but I trust in the LORD."
Psalm 31:6

Dear Jehovah,

The idols that rule this world are worth nothing. They have zero credibility. Yet, I see every day that there are still people who worship idols. They worship their phones, their books, their television, or themselves. To them, their idols are worth everything. They feel as if they cannot live without this idol, that this idol will bring everlasting life. They are foolish.

What is astounding are the most foolish—the Christians, Your people, who join the idol worshippers. It grieves You. My heart hurts for You because You give Your whole being to them and they reject You. It is a slap to the face. With boldness in faith, I state that those who worship worthless idols are deeming themselves the vain among vanities. Vanities is putting anything, something, or someone above You, Lord. The vanities grieve You. Jehovah, what is peculiar is that the vain do not even know they are indeed the ones being controlled by the vanities. The vanities are worthless, and the lying is deceitful to themselves. People need to fear You. They need to know You are a jealous God. As You spoke to Moses, "They have moved me to jealously with *that which is* not God; they have provoked me to anger with their vanities: and I will move them to jealousy with *those which are* not a people; I will provoke them to anger with a foolish nation" (Deut. 32:21).

You do not look up at idols. You don't even look down at idols because You are the One on the throne. Your focus is never on the idols themselves but on the ones who worship those idols. For idols cannot speak, move, or hear the people who worship them. Indeed, Your eyes are upon the ones that are deceived, and their eyes are upon the deceiver. Those who are deceived and worship the idols of the enemy will *never* get into the kingdom of God. Your Word is clear from the beginning: "For this ye know, that no whoremonger, nor unclean person, nor covetous man, who is an idolater, hath any inheritance in the kingdom of Christ and of God" (Eph. 5:5). Those who are idol worshippers must understand that false gods make false people, a false people who "followed vanity, and became vain" (2 Kings 17:15) and who quell the truth, "for the wrath of God is revealed from heaven against all ungodliness and unrighteousness of men, who hold the truth in unrighteousness" (Rom. 1:18), a people "who changed the truth of God into a lie, and worshipped and served the creature more than the Creator, who is blessed forever. Amen" (Rom. 1:25). Yet, You are all-powerful and all-knowing. You have no rival and no equal! You are the Creator! "For all the gods of the people *are* idols: but the LORD made the heavens" (1 Chron. 16:26).

You are the One in whom we must trust, the only One who *can* be trusted. You can be relied upon like none of the worthless idols of this world that darken the soul and heart. You are the One True King who reigns over all kingdoms and nations. Trust can be only placed in You,

Jehovah, not in people or idols. Those who place their trust in idols You curse. They turn their hearts away from You. There is no hope for their future, and their spiritual life is stunted like shrubs in the desert destined to live a barren life, one that is forsaken (see Jer. 17:5-6). To place trust in an idol is sure to be lasting devastation. The wrath of God will breathe upon their neck. As the prophet Ezekiel says, "And I will execute great vengeance upon them with furious rebukes; and they shall know that *I am* the LORD, when I shall lay my vengeance upon them" (Ezek. 25:17).

Alas, the wise know the course of the Lord. You are a just God who does not like to see His children suffer foolishly. You always give Your children a choice. That choice can be of wisdom or foolishness. Darkness or light. Wrath of God or the love of God. Sin or repentance. The choice is paramount but rather simple. God, You are the choice and the simplicity. Choosing You is choosing to repent of all sins surging toward redemption and trust in Jehovah.

> Blessed *is* the man that trusteth in the LORD, and whose hope the LORD is. For he shall be as a tree planted by the waters, and *that* spreadeth out her roots by the river, and shall not see when heat cometh, but her leaf shall be green; and shall not be careful in the year of drought, neither shall cease from yielding fruit. (Jer. 17:7-8)

Those that choose to trust in You are cleansed of their sins and will produce unyielding fruit. It is a choice made of mind, body, soul, and heart. You make it clear to never cut corners in making the choice. There is no shortcut. Your children cannot be half in and half out; they must be either all in or all out. For a fool You are not. You know all things and examine all matters.

The heart *is* deceitful above all *things*, and desperately wicked: who can know it? I the LORD search the heart, *I* try the reins, even to give every man according to his ways, *and* according to the fruit of his doings. (Jer. 17:9-10)

Your Wise Servant

Letter 7

The Mercy of the Known

"I will be glad and rejoice in thy mercy: for thou hast considered my trouble;
thou hast known my soul in adversities."
Psalm 31:7

Dear Lord,

Your mercy brings gladness and joy upon the faces of those who rejoice in You. Mercy in Hebrew is *checed*, and the meaning is quite fascinating. Strong's Concordance defines *checed* as "loving-kindness, steadfast love, grace, mercy, faithfulness, goodness, devotion." These words describe Your mercy I know that I have mentioned Jesus a lot, but, Lord, I cannot help myself. He is the channel of Your mercy. He has set me free and united me with You.

You showed me mercy when Your Son was sacrificed for me out of love, to cleanse me of my sins and to be in unity with You. This was a demonstration not only of Your love but also of Your devotion to Your fallen people. Never once have You failed me or Your people. You are always faithful, even when I sin and make mistakes, for it is by that faithfulness that mercy is accessible by Your children. It is by that faithfulness that Your children understand Your mercy.

Lord, this world needs Your mercy. Every day sin permeates the atmosphere and because of that, mercy is a necessity. Mercy is withholding merited punishment, while grace is unmerited favor. Lord, You are surely a good and awesome God! For Your mercy is compassion—compassion in action. It is loving-kindness, steadfast love, faithfulness, and devotion to Your children.

> But God, who is rich in mercy, for his great love wherewith he loved us, Even when we were dead in sins, hath quickened us together with Christ, (by grace ye are saved). (Eph. 2:4-5)

You understand that we are a fallen people. This world is corrupt. Indeed, we are treacherous people, just barely standing on the edge with Your mercy pulling us away from peril. Lord, You do not have to show us mercy. You could be cold-hearted and calculated, finally pushing us off that edge. But then that would not be You. You are holy, loving, forgiving, generous, compassionate, and merciful. By Your mercy we are sustained, we are made whole again.

God Almighty, Your mercy is not motivated by pity for us. It is motivated by love. You are the God of compassion and mercy who is slow to anger and filled with unfailing and faithful love, a love so fulfilling and holy that You forgive all iniquities, rebellions, and sins (see Exod. 34:6-7). With tears in my eyes and a grateful heart, I acknowledge that Your mercy is a gift that must not be wasted away. I must receive Your mercy in Your strength as one who has the favor of God. For I am not strong enough to receive Your mercy, especially mercy that was crucified. I am a broken individual that is not deserving of Your mercy. I need Your strength to accept the mercy that was freely crucified for me. The Apostle Paul writes,

What if God, willing to shew *his* wrath, and to make his power known, endured with much longsuffering the vessels of wrath fitted to destruction: And that he might make known the riches of his glory on the vessels of mercy, which he had afore prepared unto glory. (Rom. 9:22-23)

With Your strength, I rejoice in Your mercy that You have blessed me with.

God, You have compassion upon the suffering of my soul. For You know my soul in times of adversity. You have made the soul the most critical part of the human body. Each one is either saved or unsaved, going to heaven or hell, producing spiritual fruit or dead fruit. Jesus questions what happens to the soul living in a worldly place, "For what is man profited, if he shall gain the whole world, and lose his own soul? or what shall a man give in exchange for his soul?" (Matt. 16:26). Lord, my soul *is* crucial, and I should take notice.

First and foremost, every soul belongs to You. Yes, even an unsaved soul belongs to You, because You are judge over all. God, You say: "Behold, all souls are mine; as the soul of the father, so also the soul of the son is mine: the soul that sinneth, it shall die" (Ezek. 18:4). You are the judge of whether we go to heaven or hell. By Your mercy can a soul be made right if it fully accepts Jesus as the savior and repents of all sins.

I surrender the soul completely. For "he restoreth my soul: he leadeth me in the paths of righteousness for his name's sake" (Ps. 23:3). The soul that surrenders to You is a soul that chooses You. The souls of those who choose You are kept solely by You. You are the Keeper. You will keep it from all evil, and the soul will be preserved (see Ps. 121:7). Choosing You means obeying you. Being obedient as Moses was obedient to You. Being obedient with an undying love for You, for Your truth. "Seeing ye have purified your souls in obeying the truth through the Spirit unto unfeigned love of the brethren, *see that ye* love one another with a pure heart fervently" (1 Pet. 1:22).

The soul of my Abba brings fruitful and lasting spiritual life. My soul yearns for more of You because I was created in Your image, thus I have Your soul within me.

> As the hart panteth after the water brooks, so panteth my soul after thee, O God. My soul thirsteth for God, for the living God: when shall I come and appear before God? (Ps. 42:1-2)

And my soul, "thou shalt love the Lord thy God with all thy heart, and with all thy soul, and with all thy strength, and with all thy mind; and thy neighbour as thyself" (Luke 10:27).

Your Thankful Servant

Letter 8

"And hast not shut me up into the hand of the enemy: thou hast set my feet in a large room."
Psalm 31:8

Dear Lord My Banner,

As I was reading Your Word, I came across this title of Yours. *Jehovah Nissi*: the Lord my Banner. In ancient times, when tribes would go to battle against one another, they would carry onto the battlefield a banner that signified which tribe they belonged to, who they fought for. Just as in ancient times, I also carry Your banner into battle. Knowing that You are always by my right side, proving that my confidence comes from knowing You fight for me. I raise that banner pronouncing and declaring to the enemy that I fight by Your side and that You fight by my side. *Jehovah Nissi* is never defeated. You are always the victor! I always have the victory with faith and trust in You!

Lord, my God, You will never give me over to the enemy. You will not shut me up into the hands of the enemy. For "Blessed *be* the LORD thy God, which hath delivered up the men that lifted up their hand against my lord the king" (2 Sam. 18:28). Though to place me in Your protective hands is important, there is another word that is just as important: *hand*.

In Psalm 31:8 I pray that You "hast not shut me up into the hand of the enemy." No, Lord, You will not let the hand of the enemy capture me. Instead, with confidence I know that I am in Your hands. Your hand is strong and rules with power. I am hidden in the shadow of Your hand while You sharpen my arrows to fight the enemy (see Isa. 49:2). Holding me in Your hands is proclaiming Your power over the enemy, my enemy.

Jehovah, I know I cannot take myself in my own hands. I cannot take over matters. I can certainly not defeat the enemy on my own. If I take it into my own hands, there will be consequences detrimental to myself and my soul. The Scripture says

> And thou say in thine heart, My power and the might of *mine* hand hath gotten me this wealth. But thou shalt remember the LORD thy God: for *it is* he that giveth thee power to get wealth, that he may establish his covenant which he sware unto thy fathers, as *it is* this day. And it shall be, if thou do at all forget the LORD thy God, and walk after other gods, and serve them, and worship them, I testify against you this day that ye shall surely perish. As the nations which the LORD destroyeth before your face, so shall ye perish; because ye would not be obedient unto the voice of the LORD your God. (Deut. 8:17-20)

The hand of the enemy will never stop me because I have a God who is always for me. In fact, the hand of the enemy will be turned into the hand of *Jehovah Nissi*.

As Your children, we must let You fight our battles. We cannot do it on our own. The battle belongs to You. Fighting our own battle only leads to sorrow, destruction, and derailment from the path. Abba, it will lead to You turning Your hand upon Your children.

When I kept silence, my bones waxed old through my roaring all the day long. For day and night thy hand was heavy upon me: my moisture is turned into the drought of summer. (Ps. 32:3-4).

You are a jealous god. We must put Your ways and thoughts above our ways and thoughts. We must serve and obey You above all else. Your hands give us strength to fight the battle. You strengthen the weak hands and hearten those who have frail knees (see Isa. 35:3). Your Word says, "Thou hast a mighty arm: strong is thy hand, *and* high is thy right hand" (Ps. 89:13). The victory is distant from the enemy. We grasp the enemy by the neck, declaring we have the victory over him in Your strength. The enemy will know who stands at our right hand! "Thy hand *shall be* in the neck of thine enemies; thy father's children shall bow down before thee" (Gen. 49:8).

Most assuredly the enemy can never touch Your people because You plant their feet firmly in Your refuge. You set them in a safe place, Your shelter. When You set their feet on solid ground, You are establishing them and signifying to the enemy that Your children are immovable because You fight by their side. In the book of Joshua, when Your blessed nation Israel was being attacked by the Amorites, Joshua prayed fervently. He prayed to You in front of all the Israelites, and his prayer was to let the sun and moon stand still to defeat the enemies. Because of his belief in You, "the sun stood still, and the moon stayed, until the people had avenged themselves upon their enemies" (Josh. 10:13). Jehovah, that is the kind of power You are. You will plant Your people on firm ground, stop the sun and the moon to defeat the enemy. You will go to great lengths for Your children. "The wicked are overthrown, and *are* not: but the house of the righteous shall stand" (Prov. 12:7). Now Your children's enemies are under their feet. They have the authority given to them by the blood of Jesus to declare that every enemy is underneath their soles. Knowing in their soul that they are the head and not the tail. The enemy is crushed with the heel of their foot. The enemy will bow down before the sons and daughters of God. Your prophet Isaiah tells us, "The sons also of them that afflicted thee shall come bending unto thee; and all they that despised thee shall bow themselves down at the soles of thy feet; and they shall call thee, The city of the LORD, The Zion of the Holy One of Israel" (Isa. 60:14). There is no mistaking that when the enemy, Satan, is underneath their feet, You will crush him. Your children must know that it is *only* by Your power that the enemy is destroyed.

When Your children choose to walk by Your side, the enemy will come and bow down to Your feet (see Rev. 3:9). Then, Lord, surely they will know it is You who gave the victory. They will bow at Your feet. Yes, they will fall face down in awe and in fear of You—this is the meaning of reverence!

> And when I saw him, I fell at his feet as dead. And he laid his right hand upon me, saying unto me, Fear not; I am the first and the last: I *am* he that liveth, and was dead; and behold, I am alive for evermore, Amen; and have the keys of hell and death. (Rev. 1:17-18)

Feet are not meant to walk around aimlessly; rather, they are meant to walk with Your strength to bring the Good News of salvation. Again, the prophet Isaiah says, "How beautiful upon the mountains are the feet of him that bringeth good tidings, that publisheth peace; that bringeth good tidings of good, that publisheth salvation; that saith unto Zion, Thy God reigneth" (Isa. 52:7). You will guide our feet with the light that illuminates from Your essence, lighting the path one step at a time and never letting it grow dim or dark. You will reveal the light that is within all, that is in every step toward Your will and purpose. Lord, "Thy word *is* a lamp unto my feet, and a light unto my path" (Ps. 119:105).

Your Victor Servant

Letter 9

Distress from the Belly and Soul

"Have mercy upon me, O LORD, for I am in trouble: mine eye is consumed with grief, yea, my soul and my belly."
Psalm 31:9

Dear Abba,

In my troubles and distresses I call upon You. With a trembling voice I call upon You, but with a shout for Your mercy to fall upon me. To call for Your mercy is subjecting myself to Your truths. The truth of knowing I am the cause of my troubles and distresses. I chose self-centeredness over God-centeredness. I chose my paths instead of Your paths. Even though I know that Your ways are higher than my ways and Your thoughts are higher than my thoughts, still I chose myself. My self-centeredness is motivated by the carnality and selfishness of this world. Oh yes, I need to call upon Your mercy! Mercy is to show favor that is neither expected nor deserved. Abba, You told Moses, "I will make all my goodness pass before thee, and I will proclaim the name of the LORD before thee; and will be gracious to whom I will be gracious, and will shew mercy on whom I will shew mercy" (Exod.

33:19). I know I am being repetitive, but Your mercy is compassion in action; it is all lovingkindness and goodness. Your mercy is who You are. "Be ye therefore merciful, as your Father also is merciful" (Luke 6:36).

I call upon You! Hear my cry, Lord! I need You! I cry out to You, for You lend an ear to me. You are my God who listens and acts in compassion for His children. You are the God of mercy and compassion (see Exod. 34:6). I could not possibly stress enough how merciful and compassionate You are. Without that I would be doomed, I would be lost. When Your favor falls upon me, my enemies will be put to shame and without a doubt, I will know You are my God (see Ps. 86:17).

I only receive mercy because of Your ultimate act, the ultimate act of Jesus who is the embodiment of mercy. You sacrificed Your own Son so that I could be set free from all my sins. His blood cleanses me. You are merciful and so full of love. For it was by Your love for me that Jesus was sacrificed. Love truly does conquer all.

> But God, who is rich in mercy, for his great love wherewith he loved us, Even when we were dead in sins, hath quickened us together which Christ, (by grace ye are saved). (Eph. 2:4-5)

I must never take Your mercy for granted. Indeed, it is an insult if I do because You paid a steep price for showing Your mercy. Yet You did it out of love. By Your act of compassion, You were glorified, because Your Son rose from the dead three days later.

> *What* if God, willing to shew *his* wrath, and to make his power known, endured with much long-suffering the vessels of wrath fitted to destruction: And that he might make known the riches of his glory on the vessels of mercy, which he had afore prepared unto glory. (Rom. 9:22-23)

You get all the praise, glory, and worship that You most assuredly deserve. As Peter stresses to believers, "Blessed *be* the God and Father of our Lord Jesus Christ, which according to his abundant mercy hath begotten us again unto a lively hope by the resurrection of Jesus Christ from the dead" (1 Pet. 1:3).

Abba, help me not to see with eyes the troubles that are before me. Do not let my eyes be clouded by grief. My troubles have caused many heartbreaks. This grief brings weakness, a weakness that frightens me. Grief consumes my being where I cannot see each step my foot takes on the path. With a cloud of grief, I do not see You standing right in front of me. I cannot see Your outstretched hand beckoning me to fall into Your arms, as You call to me with Your crystal-clear eyes to surrender all to You. Lord, uncloud my eyes. They need to be unclouded, so that I may see spiritually and more clearly what You are seeing. For "Behold, the eye of the LORD *is* upon them that fear him, upon them that hope in his mercy" (Ps. 33:18). "Neither is there any creature that is not manifest in his sight: but all things *are* naked and opened unto the eyes of him with whom we have to do" (Heb. 4:13).

My Abba, my grief-stricken heart will cease to beat the rhythm of life and my soul will turn the darkest gray. Grief sucks the breath of life out of me. It encompasses both physical and emotional pain from the soul and spirit. Unrelenting grief is the sickness of mind, body, and soul. Lord, I must overcome this. I must not let the troubles and distresses turn my soul dark with grief. I must not let the darkness cloud my vision. Do not let it consume me, breaking my heart.

My Father, You have placed someone far greater in this world that has suffered more than I ever will. He has suffered more grief than I could ever possibly handle. He suffered all my bruisings, beatings, and tortures so that I could be set free from all sins. His grief for His people is so great that He voluntarily sacrificed His body for His people to be saved for all of eternity. He is the bearer of my grief and the One to heal me of all heartache because of what He went through. Isaiah says of Him,

> He is despised and rejected of men; a man of sorrows, and acquainted with grief: and we hid as it were *our* faces from him; he was despised, and we esteemed him not. Surely he hath borne our griefs, and carried our sorrows: yet we did esteem him stricken, smitten of God, and afflicted. But he *was* wounded for our transgressions, *he was* bruised for our iniquities: the chastisement of our peace *was* upon him; and with his stripes we are healed. All we like sheep have gone astray; we have turned everyone to his own way; and the LORD hath laid on him the iniquity of us all. (53:3-6)

My soul has been tortured by grief. Quite frankly, it has been tortured enough. My soul is my innermost being, the essence of life. Lord, my soul needs to be revived like Lazarus. Breathe life back into my soul, bringing joy, happiness, and healing to my grief-stricken heart. Search my soul, search the darkest parts. Certainly You will find that darkest part, turning it to light, exposing every hidden motive (see Prov. 20:27). Turn my darkness into my greatest joy. I rejoice when my grief becomes a joy. It is in You that I rejoice because You have helped me overcome grief. I will rejoice in all You have done for me! The heavens will know, and the heavens will hear my voice with the praises of You on my lips. I will rejoice with unabandoned joy! "And God shall wipe away all tears from their eyes; and there shall be no more death, neither sorrow, nor crying, neither shall there be any more pain: for the former things are passed away" (Rev. 21:4).

Your Rejoicing Servant

Letter 10

My Bones Are Consumed

"For my life is spent with grief, and my years with sighing; my strength faileth because of mine iniquity, and my bones are consumed."
Psalm 31:10

Dear God,

My mind and heart are desperately seeking, reaching for the light. My spirit and soul are repressed. A spirit and soul that is repressed is a life without air, a life of bones. This life of bones has on the flesh of grief, a grief that is unbearable and needs to be given to God. As God takes my grief His Spirit covers my bones. The Spirit becomes my life. Grief should never take one's life, should never be the bones of life. For life is the very essence of being. Life is the very being of God. The Lord "formed man *of* the dust of the ground, and breathed into his nostrils the breath of life; and man became a living soul" (Gen. 2:7).

Though I must grieve to shed my sadness, it does become a necessity. I cannot grieve to the extent that it takes over my life. That it becomes the essence of who I am. Pushing You, God out of my life. Therefore, grief becomes a choice. Life or death. Lord, this grief has forced me to choose You or myself. Through Your Word, I have come to know You. You are the One who gives me life, gives me hope, restores me. If I choose myself over You, the enemy will come and snatch away my soul. Even if I just give the enemy an inch, a smudge of my soul, my life is very much in peril. Thus, Lord, You say, "I call heaven and earth to record this day against you, *that* I have set before you life and death, blessing and cursing: therefore choose life, that both thou and thy seed may live" (Deut. 30:19). God, the choice is within my hands. My decision will mean my life or death, that is, my spiritual life or spiritual death. When I choose You, I give over all grief to You and receive Your strength, but when I turn into myself, that grief consumes me and destroys me.

A life spent with grief is a life that is shortened by sadness. Sorrow grips the heart, unrelenting in pain, a pain that can drive the mind to death. In sorrow the heart is downcast and heavy ladened. The psalmist says, "The sorrows of death compassed me, and the pains of hell gat hold upon me: I found trouble and sorrow" (Ps. 116:3). In sorrow, the heart is filled with bitterness and unending grief that bring more distresses (see Rom. 9:2). My sorrow speaks to me that I am alone in my troubles. It speaks to the darkness of my heart, calling to me that I am isolated and that no one understands what I am going through.

But, God, that is hardly true. It is an outrageous lie designed by the enemy to cut me off from You and Your people. You have designed us to experience similar trials and tribulations. Therefore, there is always someone out there who has gone through trials and troubles similar to mine. They have made it out, and they bring their testimony for me to hear the sweet song of victory that is already mine. Just as they have You, the Almighty, so have someone greater on my side. You, God, understand all. You know my sorrow; You know all my troubles. You feel my sorrow because You have known sorrow. It grieved Your heart when Adam and Eve disobeyed You. It grieved Your heart when Your people were constantly sinning resulting in wandering around the wilderness for forty years (see Ps. 78:40). And it especially grieved Your heart when Your only Son was sacrificed on the cross. Yes, You surely know sorrow. The only way to wipe the sorrow away is to rejoice in Your name, to rejoice for every blessing You have graced me with, to rejoice because I am saved by the blood of Your Son! Rejoice!

Though I rejoice in my grief, still I have many failures in my sinful nature. The strength I once had fails me because of my sins. My strength does not come from myself. I cannot by my strengths overcome my failures. Only You can do that, God. Only by the blood of my brother Jesus are my sins cleansed from my soul. I must depend solely upon Your strength, for it is "not by might, nor by power, but by my spirit, saith the LORD of hosts" (Zech. 4:6) that I shall overcome all. Even if I attempt to take hold of my strength, I will fail, because it is not I who have overcome my sins. Rather, Jesus is the One to cleanse and purify my heart. Jesus has overcome my sins. I must believe, have faith, and trust in the One who sacrificed all for me.

Though I know all of that, I still try to overcome by my own strength. Deep within my heart, I know that is a fruitless effort. But my mind attempts to reconcile the self to its former being. A former being of pride and selfishness that will stop at nothing to get its way. It is only satisfied if I succumb to the ever-increasing pressures of the world, a world that is about self: self-image, self-will, self-sufficiency, self-reliance. All these lead to failure. God, You abhor the self-made. You want me to rely solely on You. For You will never fail me, even when I fail You. You love me too much to ever fail me.

Yet You tell us what happens to those who choose their own ways. "The most proud shall stumble and fall, and none shall raise him up: and I will kindle a fire in his cities, and it shall devour all round about him" (Jer. 50:32). Yes, being self-made is a sin because we are disobeying You and failing to trust You. God, sin is an offense to Your holiness, a distortion of the truth. Those who rely on their own strength are relying on themselves. In one of Your commandments, you proclaim, "Thou shalt not bow down thyself to them, nor serve them: for I the LORD thy God *am* a jealous God, visiting the iniquity of the fathers upon the children unto the third and fourth *generation* of them that hate me" (Exod. 20:5). We *must* not serve ourselves, for then we will surely fail and are in grave danger of angering You.

God, as contrary as this might sound, I believe there *is* hope for those that fail in their strength. There *is* hope that I myself will turn away from relying upon my own strength and my sins, taking that first step on the path of holiness. There *is* hope that You, my God, will forgive me of my sins when I repent, surrendering all my strength and absorbing Your strength. You have given me the key to unlock. The key is to surrender *all* to You. Your shoulders are broad enough and strong enough to handle all my burdens. I must surrender to You my sins, my strength, my selfish ways. You want my heart. You want me to let go of what burdens my heart so that You can carry me in Your loving arms.

You are the One who gives strength because You are strength. No one is as strong and faithful as You (see Ps. 89:8). You are *El Shaddai*, the Lord Almighty. The prophet Jeremiah prayed a powerful prayer to You that describes Your might and strength,

> Ah Lord GOD! behold, thou hast made the heaven and the earth by thy great power and stretched out arm, *and* there is nothing too hard for thee: Thou shewest lovingkindness unto thousands, and recompensest the iniquity of the fathers into the bosom of their children after them: the Great, the Mighty God, the LORD of hosts, *is* his name, Great in counsel, and mighty in work: for thine eyes *are* open upon all the ways of the sons of men: to give every one according to his ways, and according to the fruit of his doings. (Jer. 32:17-19)

All strength bows to You. Even those who think their strength is greater than Yours shall bow to the One who created them. For every knee shall bow before You. "Therefore shall the strong people glorify thee, the city of the terrible nations shall fear thee" (Isa. 25:3).

God, You proclaim, "My grace is sufficient for thee: for my strength is made perfect in weakness" (2 Cor. 12:9). O God, sin is a weakness, but by Your strength, my weakness is overcome. Sin is darkness that casts a dark shadow upon Your people. It stalks us everywhere we go, and we must *always* be vigilant. Keep my eyes keen. Because "If thou doest well, shalt thou not be accepted? and if thou doest not well, sin lieth at the door. And unto thee *shall be* his desire, and thou shalt rule over him" (Gen. 4:7). I do not want to be chained, for sin is a bondage that will rule over my life. It can only reign over my life if I allow it. *If* I allow it. For "His own iniquities shall take the wicked himself, and he shall be holden with the cords of his sins" (Prov. 5:22).

Essentially, my sin is a slave driver (see John 8:34), leading me astray from the Righteous One. Oh, but the Righteous One is still on my side; it is I who turns my back on You. Even when I know You are my savior. "But the scripture hath concluded all under sin, that the promise by faith of Jesus Christ might be given to them that believe" (Gal. 3:22). By now, surely, Your people know that sin will be the very death of them—worldly and spiritual death.

Alas, the question I pose to You, Lord, is how *can* I break the bondage of sin? You lead me to Your Word to find the answer. To break the bondage of sin is repentance. That is to be forgiven. There is only one way to be forgiven: Jesus. Jesus was sacrificed so that I can be set free from the bondage of sin. Every drop of blood was for me, for us. Every bruise, beating, and torture was for me. You voluntarily sacrificed for me as an offering so that I could be forgiven and find union with You. Your victory gives me freedom from the slavery of sin.

There is therefore now no condemnation to them which are in Christ Jesus, who walk not after the flesh, but after the Spirit. For the law of the Spirit of life in Christ Jesus hath made me free from the law of sin and death. (Rom. 8:1-2)

It is by His blood that I am truly cleansed and purified from all my sins, as long as I repent. I must first take that step to You, fall face down, and repent with a sincere heart. I must hold a reverence of You. Then I must believe that the One who sacrificed for me has truly cleansed and purified me of *all*. John describes perfectly how Jesus is the cleanser and purifier,

> Whosoever committeth sin transgresseth also the law: for sin is the transgression of the law. And ye know that he was manifested to take away our sins; and in him is no sin. Whosever abideth in him sinneth not: whosoever sinneth hath not seen him, neither known him. (1 John 3:4-6)

Though my bones were covered with grief and sin, now my bones are consumed by the fire of God. My bones are covered with Your strength, Your flesh of the Holy Spirit. Lord, breathe life back into my bones like Ezekiel in the Valley of Dry Bones. For I am no longer living in a valley of death, but I am living in Your valley of life. Bones consumed by Your fire represent the essence of that individual, the essence of freedom from grief and sin. When You consume my bones by fire, You are reaching down to the deepest aspects of my being, searching and grasping for my heart to cradle it in Your loving hands with protective care. I am consumed by the fire of God deep down in my bones. Your Word says,

> Thus saith the Lord GOD; Behold, O my people, I will open

your graves, and cause you to come up out of your graves, and bring you into the land Israel. And ye shall know that I *am* the LORD, when I have opened your graves, O my people, and brought you up out of your graves, And shall put my spirit in you, and ye shall live, and I shall place you in your own land: then shall ye know that I the LORD have spoken *it*, and performed *it*, saith the LORD. (Ezek. 37:12-14)

Your Lively Bones Servant

Letter 11

Compassion for the Broken

"I was a reproach among all mine enemies, but especially among my
neighbors, and a fear to mine acquaintance: they that did see me without
fled from me."
Psalm 31:11
"I am forgotten as a dead man out of mind: I am like a broken vessel."
Psalm 31:12

Dear God of My Brokenness,

In the middle of the twelfth verse of Psalm 31, between the first part—"I am forgotten as a dead man out of mind"—and the second part—"I am like a broken vessel"—there is a dismantling of the heart. One must be broken before beauty comes from the ashes.

Three words dominate that first part: *forgotten, dead,* and *mind.* *Forgotten* indicates being lost or neglected. But You, God do not forget anyone. That includes those who are not believers of You. How could you forget us? You created us thus, You could never forget. Yes I proclaim that I am not forgotten, because You can never forget me. I do not say this with arrogance but with a heart that knows You are my

Father. "Can a woman forget her sucking child, that she should not have compassion on the son of her womb? yea, they may forget, yet will I not forget thee" (Isa. 49:15). You could never forget me, no matter how many times I have sinned. For You created me out of love and know every single hair on the top of my head. You know the set of my eyes, the dusting of freckles, the shape of my face, and the curve of my smile. You, my Creator could never forget me; You are my sculptor. In honesty, it is *I* who should never forget the Lord my God. For You have already blessed me tenfold. I will never forget You.

And can one who is not forgotten ever be dead? No, because the one that was not forgotten is surely alive and remembered by the Creator. Lord, can't Your people see? One who is dead has lost his life. But aren't You God? You are the One who gives life or death. Lord, You even say, "See now that I, *even I, am* he, and *there is* no god with me: I kill, and I make alive; I wound, and I heal: neither is *there any* that can deliver out of my hand" (Deut. 32:39). You are the ultimate ruler of life and death who reigns over all. But You grant us free will to make our own decisions. We can choose life or death, spiritual life or spiritual death.

Choosing spiritual death will *always* end in destruction. For death can creep upon anyone if they are not careful. It shows no remorse. It does not care about our race, ethnicity, or whether we're poor or rich. All it cares about is pulling us away from You who gives life; its only intent is to render our lives meaningless. We must make no mistake: this spiritual death is our enemy. God, we must not let it grasp us with its deathly grip. For Your Word says,

> I am counted with them that go down into the pit: I am as a man *that hath* no strength: Free among the dead, like the slain that lie in the grave, whom thou remembered no more: and they are cut off from thy hand. Thou hast laid me in the lowest pit, in darkness, in the deeps. (Ps. 88:4-6)

We will surely be cut off from hearing Your Voice, and Your ear will be turned away until we call out with such sincerity and humility that we have no other option but to choose spiritual life. Until that time comes, we will not hear Your Voice and we will not be able to praise You, for we will be unable to hope in Your faithfulness (see Isa. 38:18).

Death is a fox, a crafty enemy, that sets a trap caging its victims with a lock of sin (see Ps. 18:4-5).

> O death, where *is* thy sting? O grave, where *is* thy victory? The sting of death *is* sin; and the strength of sin *is* the law. (1 Cor. 15:55-56)

Lord, are not locks meant to be opened by the one who puts them there? Ultimately, we are the ones who put locks on ourselves and cage ourselves with death. God, sometimes we cannot help ourselves but crave to be caged in. It is interesting. The world screams and pushes at us to be independent of You, yet those who lead sinful lives are the ones who have locked themselves in cages. It is a scary thought. How can someone seem so free of this world and yet still be in a cage? You tell me the answer is simple. You say their hearts are caged. Their hearts are hardened—hardened against You, against Your love. They have made their choices, and now it is time for us to make our choice. Those who choose life are the ones fighting the good fight. They are being liberated, and they know that death is swallowed up in victory, and, God, You are the victor over all (see 1 Cor. 15:54).

Death may have great power, but its power can never exceed Your power. For You reign over all, and Your sovereignty is not limited to death. Death is under Your authority. These are the prophetic verses Isaiah speaks against death,

> And he will destroy in this mountain the face of the covering

cast over all people, and the veil that is spread over all people, and the veil that is spread over all nations. He will swallow up death in victory; and the LORD God will wipe away tears from off all faces; and the rebuke of his people shall he take away from off all the earth: for the LORD hath spoken *it*. (Isa. 25:7-8)

God, You will never leave me in the face of death. You will fight for me as I choose life.

Choosing life is a matter of the mind. Interestingly, *leb*, the Hebrew word for "the mind" also means "the heart." God, choosing life is not just a matter of the mind but of the heart. My heart is where my motives, feelings, and desires are. I must embrace my inner man (the Spirit). Therefore, my inner man becomes my mind and heart surrendering to the Spirit. Letting my motives, feelings, and emotions be godly. My heart can be receptive to the outer world or to You. Once again, I come to a choice: indulge in the sinful nature of the world or deny myself, pick up my cross, and come to You with an open heart.

The most important aspect of my heart is my emotions.

And thou shalt love the LORD thy God with all thine heart, and with all thy soul, and with all thy might. And these words, which I command thee this day, shall be in thine heart. (Deut. 6:5-6)

But the heart can also be filled with knowledge and wisdom, as we see in Solomon's famous prayer: "Give therefore thy servant an understanding heart to judge thy people, that I may discern between good and bad: for who is able to judge this thy so great a people?" (1 Kings 3:9). If my heart is filled with Your Word, then the heart will know what is right and what is wrong. However, my heart can be filled with bitterness, selfishness, anger, hate, rebellion, and pride. The heart can be so full of evil that it cannot see its way through the darkness without Your help. The Lord said to the prophet Ezekiel, "Because thine heart *is* lifted up, and thou hast said, *I am* a God, I sit *in* the seat of God, in the midst of the seas; yet thou *art* a man, and not God, though thou set thine heart as the heart of God" (Ezek. 28:2). I must set my heart right. I must set it right for eternity. Your eternity. If my heart is full of bitterness, anger, hurt, or evil, then I will never see Your kingdom. I will not set foot in Your heavenly realm.

I cannot control my own heart. Rather, You control my heart by my surrendering. I have free will, but my heart knows what is right and what is wrong. Yet my heart can become corrupted by the things I choose to do with my free will. That is, I ignore You who controls my heart. In King David's prayer of praise, he says, "I know also, my God, that thou triest the heart, and hast pleasure in uprightness" (1 Chron. 29:17). You will examine my heart, and You will try the heart to know whether I follow You or follow my own mind, follow the world (see Ps. 26:2). God, take me through the refinery, coming out either as gold or as the coals that started the fire. My heart is deceitful when the mind takes control. Oh, but You know all that is in the heart. For,

> The heart *is* deceitful above all *things*, and desperately wicked: who can know it? I the LORD search the heart, *I* try the reins, even to give every man according to his ways, *and* according to the fruit of his doings. (Jer. 17:9-10)

I must heed the Spirit who is my guide to fellowship with You, God. You create in me a pure heart made in Your image. When my heart is open, honest, and tender, You will transform it. You said to the prophet Ezekiel about Your people,

I will give them one heart, and I will put a new spirit within you; and I will take the stony heart out of their flesh, and will give them an heart of flesh: That they may walk in my statutes, and keep mine ordinances, and do them: and they shall be my people, and I will be their God. (Ezek. 11:19-20)

With finality, You control the heart, my Maker. And with all reverence, I declare that I love You with all my heart, and with all my soul, and with all my might.

I believe that at some point in everyone's Christian walk, they will experience an unspeakable hardship, an experience of being broken or being a lost vessel for You, God. As the psalmist expressed in verse 12, "I am like a broken vessel." I have been through it and I have seen family members go through it, Lord, but almost always the hardship turns into glory. During that brokenness, I can barely find the path, let alone see an inch in front of me. My thoughts overwhelm me to the point of giving up, and I am consumed with the process rather than the outcome. I feel trapped by my circumstances and believe that there is no way out. But You are bigger than my circumstances and bigger than my brokenness. However, it is only when my state of brokenness reaches the point that I can only call out to You—"Help me! I need You!"—that I am ready for You to fully mend my heart. That is the kind of brokenness that pushes me and Your children to You. The psalmist shouts with conviction,

The righteous cry, and the LORD heareth, and delivereth them out of all their troubles. The LORD *is* nigh unto them that are of a broken heart; and saveth such as be of a contrite spirit. (Ps. 34:17-18)

In the midst of my hardship, I have one recurring thought: *God, where are You?* But You are always there. You will never leave us, fail us, or forsake us. Our brokenness results in *fully* putting our faith and complete trust in You. You want us to come broken to You. For in that state of brokenness, You will reveal Your glory. Yes, "The sacrifices of God *are* a broken spirit: a broken and contrite heart, O God, thou wilt not despise" (Ps. 51:17). It is in our brokenness that we become humble—humble before You, humble enough to hear Your voice, humble enough to repent. And "A man's pride shall bring him low: but honour shall uphold the humble in spirit" (Prov. 29:23). Humility brings glory to You. Humility praises You through the valley and praises You on top of the mountain. In the midst of difficulty, we must praise, worship, and glorify You, for then we will have a joy for eternity.

Your Broken Servant

Letter 12

Fearless

"For I have heard the slander of many: fear was on every side: while they took counsel together against me, they devised to take away my life."
Psalm 31:13
"But I trusted in thee, O LORD: I said, Thou art my God."
Psalm 31:14

Dear God,

Fear, if I let it, consumes my whole being, my essence. It can devour the mind, heart, and soul with no remorse. Fear controls me. Fear alters me. Fear overshadows You who has already conquered. We see this in the story of Adam and Eve, where fear first came to humankind. After Adam and Eve ate from the tree of the knowledge of good and evil, their eyes were opened to sin. And that sin bred fear.

They heard the voice of the LORD God walking in the garden in the cool of the day: and Adam and his wife hid themselves from the presence of the Lord God amongst the trees of the garden. And the LORD God called unto Adam, and said unto him, Where *art* thou? And he said, I heard thy voice in the garden, and I was afraid, because I *was* naked; and I hid myself. (Gen. 3:8-10)

Lord, fear comes down to choices. I know I may seem repetitive, but it comes down to a choice that Your children need to make. They choose to let fear consume them or to surrender themselves completely over to You, who has victory over all. What we choose will determine the outcome of our circumstances. Yet fear can never conquer You who has already conquered. Though fear may overshadow You, those shadows will never take hold of You. For You are the light, and where there is light, darkness cannot exist. The light will always scatter the shadows that seem to overtake us. Fear can never grip the heart that belongs to You, the heart that belongs to the light.

A heart that belongs to You is a heart that has a reverent fear of You. To fear You is to be in awe of You, in so much awe that I would not dare to be disobedient and I would not dare to sin willfully. You are so powerful and awe-inspiring that when You speak instantly my knees drop in reverence of You. That is exactly what happened to Peter, James, and John in Matthew,

> While he yet spake, behold, a bright cloud overshadowed them: and behold a voice out of the cloud, which said, This is my beloved Son, in whom I am well pleased; hear ye him. And when the disciples heard *it*, they fell on their face, and were sore afraid. (Matt. 17:5-6)

Fear the Lord my God I surely will. You *have* conquered fear itself because of Your overwhelming joy and love. You *have* conquered fear itself when Jesus was crucified. Fearing You is trusting You.

Batach is the Hebrew word in verse 14 for the psalmist's trust in

God. It is a verb. Trust here is an action. It means to be reliant and unwary. *Batach* in You, Lord, is to first have faith in You, to believe in You. *Batach* comes when I have a relationship with You. You pursue me with unspeakable love, but it is when *I* pursue *You* that trust manifests. To trust in You means to rely upon You for *everything*. I must sacrifice all of myself for You to be the whole of me. God, I cannot trust myself, for the heart deceives. Trusting myself leads to sin and disobedience. Instead, I need my heart to reflect the psalmist's prayer:

> For I will not trust in my bow, neither shall my sword save me. But thou hast saved us from our enemies, and hast put them to shame that hated us. In God we boast all the day long, and praise thy name for ever. (Ps. 44:6-8)

God, You should be the only One within my heart and soul.

This *Batach*, this trusting in You, is the same as having faith. It is the defining virtue of a Christian. For "Jesus answered and said unto them, This is the work of God, that ye believe on him whom he hath sent" (John 6:29). Having faith is powerful and intoxicating. It is not faith itself but is the One in whom the faith is placed, that is powerful and intoxicating. Placing my faith in You is the most powerful and intoxicating decision. "Without faith *it is* impossible to please *him*: for he that cometh to God must believe he is, and that he is a rewarder of them that diligently seek him" (Heb. 11:6).

Your Fearless Servant

Letter 13

From My Enemies To My Protector

"My times are in thy hand: deliver me from the hand of mine enemies, and
from them that persecute me."
Psalm 31:15

Dear Abba,

In this life You have blessed me and I know I am not guaranteed to live to an old age. I am not even guaranteed tomorrow. I am only guaranteed today to live this life to my fullest, to love You with all my heart and soul, to worship You with my very being, and to give You all the glory You deserve. Yes, today I live, but tomorrow I cannot fathom. I cannot even see tomorrow. My time, my future is in Your hands. You are the only One who knows my past, present, and future. You are the seer. The seer of all seasons, all appointed times, and all opportunities.

Abba, You "changeth the times and the seasons: [You] removeth kings, and setteth up kings: [You] giveth wisdom unto the wise, and knowledge to them that know understanding" (Dan. 2:21). Though You are most definitely the seer of all, I still am required to fulfill my part, a part that You have called me to fulfill. This part can be accepted or rejected. I am called to be either obedient or disobedient to You, to bring harmony or disharmony within the seasons.

No matter the season, I am called to be obedient, and my obedience shapes how I handle that season. A servant's obedience brings confidence, assurance, and faith in You that the servant will reap the harvest. The prophet Jeremiah tells us, "Neither say they in their heart, Let us now fear the LORD our God, that giveth rain, both the former and the latter, in his season: he reserveth unto us the appointed weeks of the harvest" (Jer. 5:24). One who is obedient to You, Abba, is like a tree planted near a river that will always bring forth fruit for each season, always prospering. *Every* season in communion with You brings maturity, fruitfulness, and productivity. The writer of Ecclesiastes, Solomon, tells us, "To every *thing there is* a season, and a time to every purpose under the heaven" (Eccles. 3:1).

Whether I am obedient or disobedient, in Your hands my times are held. Your hands *are* powerful. Abba, You *are* powerful. You *are* Jehovah. By Your hands, blessings or curses can be let loose, and one can be favored or not favored. Most importantly, it is by Your right hand that one has the victory. For You to grab me by Your right hand is to occupy a position of recognition, esteem, and favor. Your badge I wear, proclaiming I am highly favored. Yes, Your Word says,

And when I saw him, I fell at his feet as dead. And he laid his right hand upon me, saying unto me, Fear not; I am the first and the last: I *am* he that liveth, and was dead; and, behold, I am alive for evermore, Amen; and have the keys of hell and of death. (Rev. 1:17-18)

Your right hand rescues and sustains me. You are God! Yes, O Lord, "shew thy marvellous lovingkindness, O thou that savest by thy right hand them which put their trust *in thee* from those that rise up *against them*" (Ps. 17:7).

Sometimes, I forget that You reign over all. Sometimes my defenses come down and my enemy attacks. Sometimes I let the enemy guide me by his right hand and I surrender my authority over to him. Abba, sometimes I am just too weak to fight back. But, my God, You are there! You are bigger than my biggest enemy! You are fighting my battles for me! You will never let me firmly grab hold of Satan's right hand. John describes the powerful rule of God saying, "My Father, which gave *them* me, is greater than all; and no *man* is able to pluck *them* out of my Father's hand" (John 10:29). Oh yes, do not let the enemy take away my authority; do not let the enemy seal my lips. I declare with the evangelist John that "the Father loveth the Son, and hath given all things into his hand" (John 3:35).

I speak these words into existence against the enemy declaring my victory over him: "Through the tender mercy of our God; whereby the dayspring from on high hath visited us, To give light to them that sit in darkness and *in* the shadow of death, to guide our feet into the way of peace" (Luke 1:78-79).

My enemies come from all sides. They are in constant action. These enemies oppose You and align themselves against Your purposes and will. The greatest enemy of all is Satan. O Lord, I must not fear, for if I am truly aligned with You then You have already "saved them from the hand of him that hated *them,* and redeemed them from the hand of the enemy" (Ps. 106:10). To not fear is to know deep in my heart that You are my warrior and my victor; You are *Jehovah Nissi.* A divine warrior are You, and no victory comes without Your help, "for the LORD your God *is* he that goeth with you, to fight for you against your enemies, to save you" (Deut. 20:4). The enemy has no authority over me because I am covered by the blood of Jesus Christ. I am covered by Your wings, by Your shadow. The enemy has no authority because I am at Your right hand. He has no authority because he is already defeated. He has *no* authority because I *believe.*

What a grievous thing it is to lose all hope in You, to disobey You. A deceiver of one's own heart makes ashes of one's own soul. A heart that becomes an enemy of You is a heart that You become an enemy of. Lord, You even became an enemy to your chosen people the Israelites, "But they rebelled, and vexed his holy Spirit: therefore he was turned to be their enemy, *and* he fought against them" (Isa. 63:10). You are a jealous God, and the fires from heaven will come down on Your enemies. You will never be crossed, for You are truly the Almighty God who knows all. However, those that are for You, You will be an enemy to their enemies. Being for You is heeding Your voice and knowing without a shadow of a doubt that You are for me, not against me. You are my victor and my defender, not my accuser. In Exodus You had sent Your angel ahead of Your people to guide them and You specifically spoke to them saying, "But if thou shalt indeed obey his voice, and do all that I speak; then I will be an enemy unto thine enemies; and an adversary unto thine adversaries" (Exod. 23:22).

My accusers are my persecutors. They are as much my enemy as they are Your enemy. Abba, those that persecute me are persecuting You! The accusers will come with a fury, with a zeal, "but not according to knowledge" (Rom. 10:2). These accusers do not know You. They cannot reconcile how a God can let people die but also be a God who is loving. What they don't know is that You give all of us free will. That free will results in a falling-dominoes of choices and those who are placed in positions of power can cause catastrophes of annihilation.

I see these accusers having a spirit of animosity in their hearts, fueled by hating their Creator, but it is just a smoke screen. Satan is the true accuser. His heart is full of rancor against You and Your people. But I must never fear, for Your wrath is unrelenting toward them. For "He hath bent his bow like an enemy: he stood with his right hand as an adversary, and slew all *that were* pleasant to the eye in the tabernacle of the daughter of Zion: he poured out his fury like fire" (Lam. 2:4). Then Your Word turns on a dime and the unthinkable happens. You allow Your people to be persecuted by those who hate You.

Your people are persecuted to bring glory to You, for Your will to be fulfilled. This will undoubtedly refine us. You receive glory through persecution because we know that it is You who reigns supreme over all, that no matter what happens to us You are King over our hearts, that we give You the glory in our suffering just as Jesus did. Jesus suffered not only to bring salvation and unity to all but to glorify His Father, our Father; to let Your will, not our will, be done. Apostle Paul describes our suffering best, saying, "Unto you it is given in the behalf of Christ, not only to believe on him, but also to suffer for his sake" (Phil. 1:29).

Persecution comes for us to deny ourselves, to deny this world and our outer self. Just as Jesus said to His disciples,

> If any *man* will come after me, let him deny himself, and take up his cross, and follow me. For whosoever will save his life shall lose it: and whosoever will lose his life for my sake shall find it. (Matt. 16:24-25)

You are sifting those that are faithful from the faithless, showing that the faithful will not turn against You in times of tribulation. For again Jesus says to us,

> Blessed *are* they which are persecuted for righteousness' sake: for theirs is the kingdom of heaven. Blessed are ye, when *men* shall revile you, and persecute *you*, and shall say all manner of evil against you falsely, for my sake. Rejoice, and be exceeding glad: for great *is* your reward in heaven: for so persecuted they the prophets which were before you. (Matt. 5:10-12)

Persecution is for those who commit themselves to You with all their heart and soul. You want a relationship with us, and we desperately need that relationship. We need You. You do not pay heed to deceitful people. You are looking for people who are willing to be refined, to fulfill Your will through persecution, to go through the fire to become gold, to stand in the darkness to let Your light shine. Through the refinement, You are always there, calling us by our name as we glorify You. For, Lord, You have already spoken, "I will bring the third part through the fire, and will refine them as silver is refined, and will try them as gold is tried: they shall call on my name, and I will hear them: I will say, It *is* my people: and they shall say, The LORD *is* my God" (Zech. 13:9).

Your Obedient Servant

Letter 14

Shine upon Your Servant

"Make thy face to shine upon thy servant: save me for thy mercies' sake."
Psalm 31:16

Dear God,

In the Bible, there are only a few people who have truly seen Your face. Your servant Jacob is one of them. As he was preparing to meet Esau, his brother whom he stole his birthright from, he became increasingly worried that Esau would attack. Throughout the day worry and fear gnawed on him and when night came, he became distressed. It was during that night where Jacob met You, Lord. You wrestled with him which resulted in his name being changed to Israel and him seeing Your face. Thus Jacob said, "I have seen God face to face, and my life is preserved" (Gen. 32:30). Another is Moses, in which You, God would meet him face to face in the Tabernacle to give all Your commands towards Your people. God, You said, "And there I will meet with thee, and I will commune with thee from above the mercy seat." (Exod. 25:22).

To see Your face is to have Your favor. After seeing Your face, Your servants Jacob and Moses were favored. You preserved Jacob's life by changing his name to Israel and multiplying his descendants; Moses was chosen by You to deliver messages to the people. Through it all, You were glorified. I see that You will only show *Your* favor to those that will glorify You alone. I cannot have a heart that glorifies myself. A heart that glorifies self is a heart that has no room for You. You get all the glory or none. Your favor will shine upon those who are humble, with a servant's heart. It is a favor that will outshine all that comes against me. Your favor upon me will be as bright as the stars created by You.

To receive that favor, my heart must be a servant's heart, in which You alone are glorified. Servanthood is a characteristic of those who are called by You. As You proclaim, "For unto me the children of Israel *are* servants; they *are* my servants whom I brought forth out of the land of Egypt: I *am* the LORD your God" (Lev. 25:55). Emphatically, You do not call upon the proud and selfish. You call upon the humble and meek of heart. You call upon the ones who are all for You. Your servants want to serve, not to be served. To have a servant's heart is to be obedient. One who is obedient will see Your favor fall upon them. As Paul wrote to the Christians of Corinth,

> Let a man so account of us, as of the ministers of Christ, and stewards of the mysteries of God. Moreover, it is required in stewards, that a man be found faithful. (1 Cor. 4:1-2)

First and foremost, I must not put labels on my heart or my soul. I must declare that I am Your servant just as Jesus was. Jesus, Your Son, was the epitome of a model servant. From washing the feet of His disciples to sacrificing His body for all, there has been no greater servant than Jesus. Your prophet Isaiah foreshadowed his coming when he proclaimed, "Behold, my servant shall deal prudently, he shall be exalted and extolled, and be very high" (Isa. 52:13). Since I am a servant of You, God, I am also a servant of Christ. Therefore, Christ is my Lord. "Ye call me Master and Lord: and ye say well; for *so* I am" (John 13:13). To be a servant of Christ, I must not come with the heart seeking to be served but to serve others, and I must be willing to give up my life for many. God, it is a hard thing to comprehend, let alone to do. I must be a living and holy sacrifice that is a pleasing aroma unto You. A servant of Christ does not just serve others and sacrifice all, but a servant of Christ *worships* the Lord Almighty. This servant *is* a pleasing aroma to the Lord.

Worshipping You means offering praise and glory to You. Serving You brings forth worshipping You. As I serve You with delight, then joy comes in Your presence. Serving others brings a joy in the heart that can only burst with passion for You, God. A passion that will gather people and kingdoms to worship You (see Ps. 102:2), singing and shouting heavenly praises with an uplifting, sweet aroma. This serving and worship *must* only be for Jehovah. As Jesus said, "Get thee behind me, Satan: for it is written, Thou shalt worship the Lord thy God, and him only shalt thou serve" (Luke 4:8).

As Your servant, I must not give sway to the prideful streak inside of me by claiming glory for myself. For "who changed the truth of God into a lie, and worshipped and served the creature more than the Creator, who is blessed forever. Amen" (Rom. 1:25). Such a servant may be common in this world, but those who serve to give glory to You will be known. As the prophet Malachi states, "Then shall ye return, and discern between the righteous and the wicked, between him that serveth God and him that serveth him not" (Mal. 3:18).

In servanthood is worship that brings You everlasting love. An everlasting love that ushers in Your mercy. Mercy is lovingkindness, faithfulness, and steadfast love. It is love ever loyal to us. It is a relationship on the foundation of truth and faithfulness. Your mercy is compassion in action that results in the fulfillment of Your promises. As You told us through your prophet Isaiah, "Incline your ear and come unto me: hear, and your soul shall live; and I will make an everlasting covenant with you, *even* the sure mercies of David" (Isa. 55:3). The fulfillment of Your promises will never depart from us because of Your great mercy. Through Isaiah You speak thus, "For the mountains shall depart, and the hills be removed; but my kindness shall not depart from thee, neither shall the covenant of my peace be removed, saith the LORD that hath mercy on thee" (Isa. 54:10). It is one of the astounding characteristics that You show Your people continuously. You will surely let all know the kind of God You are, as you did before Moses: "And the LORD passed by before him, and proclaimed, The LORD, The LORD God, merciful and gracious, longsuffering, and abundant in goodness and truth" (Exod. 34:6).

As I have said, Jesus was Your greatest servant, but He was more than just a servant unto You. He was *the* merciful servant. It is through Jesus that we see Your mercy become embodied and displayed in action. The sacrifice of Your Son unveiled Your great mercy.

But God, who is rich in mercy, for his great love wherewith he loved us, Even when we were dead in sins, hath quickened us together with Christ, (by grace ye are saved). (Eph. 2:4-5)

You do not have to show us mercy, but because You *are* love, that mercy will forever come through Jesus. For "So then *it is* not of him that willeth, nor of him that runneth, but of God that sheweth mercy" (Rom. 9:16).

As You show mercy to me thus, I am to show mercy unto others. For You require of me to do what is just with mercy and to walk humbly before You (see Mic. 6:8). Showing mercy to others is an act of compassion that is planted in my heart by You. If I do not show mercy to others, then I will not be shown mercy, for You bless those who are merciful.

As You are patient, slow to anger, and loving, so must I be, for I was created by You, God, in Your image. Your Word says,

> *What* if God, willing to shew *his* wrath, and to make his power known, endured with much longsuffering the vessels of wrath fitted to destruction: And that he might make known the riches of his glory on the vessels of mercy, which he had afore prepared unto glory. (Rom. 9:22-23)

Mercy flows from the soul that the Holy Spirit consumes with fire. I now see that mercy is in each and every one of us. We just have to make the choice, for You already made Your choice for us:

> But ye *are* a chosen generation, a royal priesthood, an holy nation, a peculiar people; that ye should shew forth the praises of him who hath called you out of darkness into his marvelous light; Which in time past *were* not a people, but *are* now the people of God: which had not obtained mercy, but now have obtained mercy. (1 Pet. 2:9-10)

Your Worshipping Servant

Letter 15

The Wicked Are Shamed

"Let me not be ashamed, O LORD; for I have called upon thee: let the wicked be ashamed, and let them be silent in the grave."
Psalm 31:17

Dear Lord,

To call upon You is to seek You. As the prophet Amos spoke, *"Seek him that maketh the seven stars and Orion, and turneth the shadow of death into the morning, and maketh the day dark with night: that calleth for the waters of the sea, and poureth them out upon the face of the earth: The LORD is his name"* (Amos 5:8). You want us to seek You, and we urgently need You. Lord, You have already found us; it is now our turn to respond to the conversation. We have to take that step toward You. You hear those who desperately seek You with all their hearts and souls. Lord, You have no bias.

Lord, You tell me to come just as I am. To come broken, ashamed, and dying. In the seventh century B.C., your servant King Hezekiah prayed for the people who failed to cleanse themselves in the required ritual washing before eating the Passover meal. And because Hezekiah sought You, Lord, You heard his prayer and pardoned them.

But Hezekiah prayed for them saying, The good LORD pardon every one *That* prepareth his heart to seek God, the LORD God of his fathers, though *he be* not *cleansed* according to the purification of the sanctuary. And the LORD hearkened to Hezekiah, and healed the people. (2 Chron. 30:18-20)

You used Hezekiah to demonstrate how You want Your people to come to You. You are my redeemer, my healer, my cleanser. I must seek You earnestly, and I shall not be ashamed of my earnest seeking. You hear my cries and prayers. I know that You are constantly seeking Your people, never missing anything.

To not be ashamed by the wicked is to proclaim with confidence what dwells in my heart: "O God, thou *art* my God; early will I seek thee: my soul thirsteth for thee, my flesh longeth for thee in a dry and thirsty land, where no water is" (Ps. 63:1). God, You are my gardener. You water and cultivate my dry soul, heart, and mouth to speak forth. I am an overgrown rose bush that seeks my gardener. Prune me, Lord, so my thorns are Your weapons and so that I can speak to the wicked, "It is my God who can only quench my thirst, who purifies my heart with His fire!" Oh, the wicked have many fiery arrows that know all my weaknesses and faults, but I must fight back with Your fiery sword. The wicked study their opponents and their attacks are calculated. I must strategize to fight back. I have to study my opponent and know all their weaknesses.

The wicked know no peace, and they corrupt the king's court until they are removed so that his throne may be "established in righteousness" (Prov. 25:5). The wicked are hostile toward You and Your people; they seek to debase the righteous. But God, You tell us, "They that forsake the law praise the wicked: but such as keep the law contend with them" (Prov. 28:4). One who is wicked desires evil; his mouth speaks venom, turning the heart to be unjust. Yet even though the wicked are vile, they have already been defeated, conquered by You, Yahweh. I claim that victory in Your name. I have faith and confidence in You. To know You are *my Jehovah Nissi*.

To defeat the wicked, I first have to fight the wicked. But I *must* fight with urgency, an urgency like my soul is being consumed by the fire of the Holy Spirit. I *must* fight like I am the Lion of Judah. God, You have given me all that I need to fight back: the breastplate of righteousness, the helmet of salvation, the shoes of peace, the shield of faith, and the sword of the Spirit. To fight against the wicked, I need to cast out all fear and know that they do have weaknesses, for "the wicked flee when no man pursueth: but the righteous are bold as a lion" (Prov. 28:1) and they "*are* like the troubled sea, when it cannot rest, whose waters cast up mire and dirt. *There is* no peace, saith my God, to the wicked" (Isa. 57:20-21). The wicked are afraid; their souls are corrupted while Your people are bold in their faith and know what their judgment is. Your people are at rest even through the storms, while the wicked cannot see through the mire and dirt; their eyes know only darkness. I can use these weaknesses against them, firm in who I am and in the foundation of Yahweh.

The wicked are defeated at last by Your hand, Lord. The psalmist understands that everyone is taken into account for their actions.

> Wherefore doth the wicked contemn God? he hath said in his heart, Thou wilt not require *it*. Thou hast seen *it*; for thou beholdest mischief and spite, to requite *it* with thy hand: the poor committeth himself unto thee; thou art the helper of the fatherless. (Ps. 10:13-14)

You hold everything in Your hands; You are the conqueror and the victor. You are the One to bless or curse. I surely never forget who holds me and who hears me. "The LORD *is* far from the wicked: but he heareth the prayer of the righteous" (Prov. 15:29).

Your Warrior Servant

Letter 16

Darkness Put to Silence

"Let the lying lips be put to silence; which speaks grievous things proudly and contemptuously against the righteous."
Psalm 31:18

Dear Abba,

The righteous will always let the darkness lie silent. Silence communicates. It communicates faithlessness (see Esther 4:14), defeat (see Isa. 47:5), and death (see Ps. 115:17). Abba, silence symbolizes darkness. The silence of darkness is death—spiritual death and sometimes physical death. When darkness surrounds me, my eyes become clouded, and I cannot see the way. Those that lie in darkness cannot hear You; they cannot hear the clarity of Your words. To their ears, Your words are garbled and distorted to fit the darkness inside their hearts, to fit their own truth, not *the Truth*.

When Jesus was taken into custody to be tried, He came before the high priest to be questioned. Mark tells us of the false witness borne against Him:

> We heard him say, I will destroy this temple that is made
> with hands, and within three days I will build another made
> without hands. But neither so did their witness agree together.
> And the high priest stood up in the midst, and asked Jesus,
> saying, Answerest thou nothing? what *is it which* these witness
> against thee? But he held his peace, and answered nothing.
> (Mark 14:58-61)

Jesus did not answer because He knew their hearts. Jesus knew that darkness was within and that to answer them would only turn them more against Him, lead them to distort His words further. His silence revealed His power and authority. Jesus's silence communicated that He is Your Son and that He is at Your right hand, sitting on the throne.

With Your wisdom, You have taught me that there is a time to speak and a time to be silent. There is a time to fight with words and a time to fight with silence. In essence, my silence conveys Your strength, Your power, Your authority, and Your eternity. It is in the silence of my prayers that I truly hear You speak with clarity, that I hear You fight, and that I hear You shout in victory. The psalmist declares this victory,

> Whoso privily slandereth his neighbour, him will I cut off:
> him that hath an high look and a proud heart will not I suffer.
> Mine eyes *shall be* upon the faithful of the land, that they may
> dwell with me: he that walketh in a perfect way, he shall serve
> me. He that worketh deceit shall not dwell within my house:
> he that telleth lies shall not tarry in my sight. (Ps. 101:5-7)

Within my silence dwells a peace and confidence that is a beacon of light casting out the darkness. Even when the darkness speaks haughtily, spitefully, and selfishly, the silence will not be shaken, will not break formation.

When the darkness becomes too much to bear, it will be one of the hardest challenges I will face. This darkness ushers in the bleakness of pride. Lord, pride is disregard for You, a defiance of You. Pride is worshipping myself above You. Through your prophet Ezekiel, You announced to the prince of Tyrus his deceitful and prideful heart: "Because thine heart *is* lifted up, and thou hast said, I *am* a God, I sit *in* the seat of God, in the midst of the seas; yet thou *art* a man, and not God, though thou set thine heart as the heart of God" (Ezek. 28:2). But You did not simply tell the prince he is just a man; You judged the prince of Tyrus justly:

> Therefore thus saith the Lord GOD; Because thou hast set thine heart as the heart of God; Behold, therefore I will bring strangers upon thee, the terrible of the nations: and they shall draw their swords against the beauty of thy wisdom, and they shall defile thy brightness. They shall bring thee down to the pit, and thou shalt die the deaths of *them that are* slain in the midst of the seas. Wilt thou yet say before him that slayeth thee, I *am* God? but thou *shalt be* a man, and no God, in the hand him that slayeth thee. Thou shalt die the deaths of the uncircumcised by the hand of strangers: for I have spoken *it*, saith the Lord God. (Ezek. 28:6-10)

You are a jealous God and there is no rival or equal to You. There is no other God but You, Jehovah.

Pride brings shame (see Prov. 11:2), breeds quarrels (Prov. 13:10), destroys (Prov. 16:18), and brings humiliation (Prov. 29:23). Pride is my enemy. Proverbs states that, "Pride goeth before destruction, and an haughty spirit before a fall" (Prov. 16:18).

But pride can be overcome. It can be overcome by You, Lord. Instead of turning and looking into myself, I must turn and look toward You.

For You are the conqueror of all! As the prophet Amos has said, "The Lord GOD hath sworn by himself, saith the LORD the God of hosts, I abhor the excellency of Jacob, and hate his palaces: therefore will I deliver up the city with all that is therein" (Amos 6:8). The prideful cannot run away from You. You run straight to them and crush them with Your mighty hand. *"For* the sin of their mouth *and* the words of their lips let them even be taken in their pride: and for cursing and lying *which* they speak" (Ps. 59:12).

You take everything away, leaving only one thing: You. You bring the high and mighty to their knees before You. On their knees, in utter despair, they lift their eyes to You. In the reflection of their eyes, one can see the shame that was wrought. They become remorseful and turn their hearts to repentance. The heart starts to beat, again and again, growing stronger with every knowing second that it was because of You, God, who saw them through. The unthinkable happens. One knee bends, then the other, until both are on the floor and arms are open wide, calling upon You. You hear and You see. The heart is home. Praising, worshipping, and glorifying You only.

Your Light Servant

Letter 17

Grandeur

"Oh how great is thy goodness, which thou hast laid up for them that fear thee; which thou hast wrought for them that trust in thee before the sons of men!"

Psalm 31:19

Dear Greatness and Goodness,

Grand. Magnificent. Awesome. Extravagant. Abundant in greatness and goodness. God, You are all of this and more. So much more. You are so much more that I do not have enough breath to say all the ways. Some of the most common characteristics I hear to describe You is greatness and goodness. The two are distinctly different. Greatness speaks volumes of Your sovereignty while goodness is love and softness. Greatness is unattainable perfection while goodness is attainable through the heart and soul molded into Your image.

Greatness is Your sovereignty and power over all things. It is promising Abraham nations and many descendants; it is splitting the Red Sea in half; it is breathing life back into dry bones; it is sacrificing Your Son, then raising Him back up three days later; and it is redeeming persecutor Saul to missionary Paul. And yet greatness is even more than this. Greatness *is* abundance in You. It is having abundance in all I do, abundance in worshipping and obeying You.

As I worship You, I seek to obey You. Obedience is necessary; it is formed out of an intimacy, a relationship, with You, God. Obedience brings fruitfulness and spiritual goodness. Spiritual goodness is my relationship with You. It is understanding who You are and who I am in Your eyes. Spiritual goodness brings Your steadfast love—"But as for me, I will come *into* thy house in the multitude of thy mercy" (Ps. 5:7)—and Your power—"Great *is* our Lord, and of great power: his understanding *is* infinite" (Ps. 147:5). I must not mistake spiritual goodness for goodness itself. For spiritual goodness is Your greatness. I cannot achieve Your perfect spiritual goodness myself. Only You can do that.

Although greatness is a noun, in You it is a verb, an action of being. It is an action that only You can reach. I cannot physically or spiritually attain Your greatness because I am not God. It is out of my reach. I can try to be great or be abundant, but every single time I will fail. Greatness is unattainable because of the sin I live with every day. I constantly have to worship You, obey You, pray to You, praise You, and glorify You. Then, God, You will be my abundance. You will be my abundance in grace, for as Paul wrote, "They which receive abundance of grace and of the gift of righteousness shall reign in life by one, Jesus Christ" (Rom. 5:17). And you will be my abundance in faith, for "your faith groweth exceedingly, and the charity of every one of you all toward each other aboundeth" (2 Thess. 1:3). It is You who chooses to be great for me because I need it. As Jesus tells us, "I am come that they might have life, and that they might have *it* more abundantly" (John 10:10).

Goodness is the awe of the Lord. It is the reverence of You, God Almighty. You are Goodness. "He is the Father, the Son, and the Holy Spirit that *are* good, *do* good, and *create* good."[5] It is in Your nature that is also in my nature. You created me in Your image; therefore, Your goodness is my goodness. Lord, You have already declared over me, "I will make all my goodness pass before thee, and I will proclaim the name of the LORD before thee." (Exod. 33:19). God, You have given me Your goodness and You have called me Your own, imprinting on me that *I* am Yours. I am chosen to carry Your goodness within my heart, to share with others the very essence of You. It is not me who is good, but I become capable of doing good by the power and presence of the Holy Spirit through the blood of Jesus Christ.

Your goodness is everywhere. There is goodness in abundance (see Exod. 34:6), in endurance (Ps. 52:1), in satisfaction (Ps. 65:4), in spiritual blessing (Ps. 31:19), in rejoicing (Exod. 18:9), and in remembrance (Ps. 145:7). Goodness is even in greatness (Ps. 31:19). Abba, what is interesting is that goodness can be tasted and seen. Two of my five senses must be active in receiving, fulfilling, and gifting Your goodness to others. The giver must first be near to You, must first trust, and must first declare all Your goodness before the giver can bear the gift. You are the Promise Keeper of every gift. Your goodness will never fail nor abandon me. For "Blessed *be* the LORD, that hath given rest unto his people Israel, according to all that he promised: there hath not failed on word of all his good promise, which he promised by the hand of Moses his servant" (1 Kings 8:56). The gift of Your goodness will always be known by Your people. By the Holy Spirit goodness flows. As the prophet Micah exclaims, "He hath shewed thee, O man, what *is* good; and what doth the LORD require of thee, but to do justly, and to love mercy, and to walk humbly with thy God" (Mic. 6:8).

In Your very being, You *are* goodness. You *do* goodness. I see it all around me, in the flowers, the mountains, the sun, the stars, and in my own beautiful soul. For "*I had fainted*, unless I had believed to see the goodness of the LORD in the land of the living" (Ps. 27:13). It is the goodness of You, Lord, that always prevails and that brings the vibrant colors of life alive. Yes, Abba, "Thou *art* good, and doest good; teach me thy statutes" (Ps. 119:68). You bring *my eyes* to the wonderful colors of life, warming my heart. I share and express to others Your goodness that will undoubtedly change their lives. Abba, Your goodness will *always* be overflowing with love, the same love that I have in my heart, bringing forth joy, happiness, forgiveness, praise, and, yes, love to others. "For every creature of God *is* good, and nothing to be refused, if it be received with thanksgiving" (1 Tim. 4:4).

Your goodness is stored up in a well of fear—not the scary, evil kind of fear, but the overwhelming, reverent kind of fear, a reverence that is only for You who is to be worshipped daily with heart and soul. Fearing You, Lord, is the climax of awe and honor that only You are worthy of. For You are the Almighty God, King of the Throne, and Creator over *all* things. At the heart of my reverence is faith and obedience, faith in my Friend who has never failed me nor abandoned me. You have sacrificed much for me to be Your child. You sacrificed Your Son so that I may be Your daughter. "Henceforth I call you not servants; for the servant knoweth not what his lord doeth: but I have called you friends; for all things that I have heard of my Father I have made known unto you" (John 15:15).

My faith, my trust in You is the awesomeness of You strumming a new tune of praise in my heart, a heart that is *always* meant to glorify You through reverence. It is when I trust You the most that I see Your trust in me. It is when the fear of You, Lord, transforms into trust in You that my eyes become opened to Your goodness. Being faithful is being obedient to You. Being obedient is more than just staying out of trouble; it is a commitment, a relationship, and a commandment to You. Obedience is giving my whole self, my whole heart, and my whole soul. It is serving only You above my desires and living by the words of Moses to the Israelites:

Now, Israel, what doth the LORD thy God require of thee, but to fear the LORD thy God, to walk in all his ways, and to love him, and to serve the LORD thy God with all thy heart and with all thy soul, To keep the commandments of the LORD, and his statutes, which I command thee this day for thy good? Behold, the heaven and the heaven of heavens *is* the LORD's thy God, the earth *also*, with all that therein *is.* (Deut. 10:12-14)

Yes, being obedient to You swells the heart with abundant laughter and joy, driving me ever closer to the goodness of You.

Closely tied to obedience, so much that they seem one and the same, is serving You. The fear of You *is* serving You with wisdom. Oh yes, wisdom is what I truly need. It is my foundation, because where there is wisdom, there is faith and there is obedience to You. A wisdom to choose to give my heart and wisdom to honor the One who cradles my heart. Wisdom is the root of my growing oak. The psalmist brings wisdom to me when he proclaims, "The fear of the LORD *is* the beginning of wisdom: a good understanding have all they that do *his commandments*: his praise endureth for ever" (Ps. 111:10). Knowing my Creator, knowing who You are and whose You are, brings divine wisdom. A pearl of divine wisdom that is captured by the heart of the humble, the heart of Jesus, the One who is wisdom. The blood of Jesus is the blood of the humble that is the cleansing divine wisdom. Thus, "The fear of the LORD *is* the instruction of wisdom; and before honour *is* humility" (Prov. 15:33).

To fear You is to be fully committed to You, to dance the same dance with You, to be in sync with You. It is gliding one foot after another in the same measure and grace as You. The Lord said through the prophet Malachi, "My covenant was with [Levi] of life and peace; and I gave them to him *for* the fear wherewith he feared me, and was afraid before my name" (Mal. 2:5). Commitment means loving what You love and hating what You hate. Lord, that means hating evil and all that is materialistic. Yes, even hating pride, conceit, and anything that is against Christ (see Prov. 8:13). By Your Word, You have taught us that "by mercy and truth iniquity is purged: and by the fear of the LORD *men* depart from evil" (Prov. 16:6). So I must do what is righteous by what You have placed in my heart, not what the enemy has distracted me with.

Oh, but Lord, every day I do see the evil that emanates from the streets, homes, and the people I love. But I must not give in. I must keep the truth of loving what You love and hating what You hate. If I do not keep Your truth, I will become what You hate. If I do not keep Your truth there will be no blessings, no Friend, no cleansing of the sins, and surely no mercy. Oh, but there is hope for the hopeless. "In every nation he that feareth him, and worketh righteousness, is accepted with him" (Acts 10:35). I must have peace and know who my God is. My peace grows stronger in Jesus Christ, the One I fear with a joy that bubbles up. I have a love that He loves and a joy in which He rejoices.

There is hope in trusting in You, trusting in Your goodness, God, a goodness that will be known throughout all kingdoms and nations. First, I *must* trust in You before I can produce the fruit of goodness. To trust someone or something is "to put one's confidence in." However, trust can be misguided by the wrong entities or can be guided by the Your right hand, Abba. Trust should never be put in weapons or in my comfort place. I must not trust my erected walls or my barbed tongue, because they will not save me (see Ps. 44:6). Even leaders of the world cannot be trusted, especially a leader who claims they are doing the Lord's work. Lord, Your Word says to always test the Spirit (see 1 John 4:1). I surrender to letting You be the judge of that leader and letting You lead me to understand who that leader is. I am not saying all leaders are not doing Your will; I am saying I should not trust a leader just because he or she says they are doing Your will. I must always test the Spirit, because You are the One I must trust.

This leads to my next point, Lord—that I must not trust in people. That is, I do not trust that any person can get me through any circumstance or that any person is the hero to solve my crisis. Forgetting this is how people can become idols. As You said to Jeremiah, "Cursed *be* the man that trusteth in man, and maketh flesh his arm, and whose heart departeth from the LORD" (Jer. 17:5).

One more thing, Lord. Your Word tells me not to put my trust in my own works and accomplishments, because then pride and selfishness will surely enter the heart. A heart that is corrupted is a heart that despises You. Though You will not take Your eyes off me, You will surely become my enemy and let my enemy take me captive. Abba, I need to be careful what I put my trust in, for I will produce what I trust.

Trust can be guided by You, but I must *choose* to trust in You by surrendering all. Lord, You have guided me to three things that I should trust: Your name (who You are), Your Word, and Jesus Christ my savior.

Focusing on Your name is how I come to know who You are. You revealed Yourself to Moses as Jehovah:

> And God spake unto Moses, and said unto him, I *am* the LORD: And I appeared unto Abraham, unto Isaac, and unto Jacob, by *the name* of God Almighty, but by name JEHOVAH was I not known to them. (Exod. 6:2-3)

Your name describes Your character. The Hebrew word, Jehovah, suggests presence, strength, power, and authority. God is Your name. In which, "Our heart shall rejoice in him, because we have trusted in his holy name" (Ps. 33:21). Before Your name, kingdoms and nations tremble. By Your name, You are known by all. And by Your name, the enemy is already slain. Oh yes, Lord, Your name is the One in which I can trust, the One I can speak with confidence and power, the One that can transform the hardened heart. You *are* most trustworthy.

Your Word is sacred. It brings truth, righteousness, salvation, strength, power, authority, protection, refuge, healing, and goodness. Your Word is what I must seek the most. It will confirm Your blessings, Your promises, and Your covenants. Your Word brings me closer to You than ever before. My relationship with You becomes stronger, and I become more certain of who You are and whose I am. It is a Word that is trustworthy from generation to generation, never fading and never deceitful. Your Word was written by the guidance of the Holy Spirit. That same Spirit confirms the trustworthiness of Your Word in my heart and soul. The words I see help me understand Your existence, and my experience of You confirms who my God is, whose I am. Your Word brought forth around the world the crucified Christ, the Good News.

Trusting in Your name and Your Word is thus trusting in Jesus Christ. He is the One who was sacrificed for me so that I can be cleansed and unified with You by the Holy Spirit. Jesus is *everything* the Word has spoken. His character is the same as Yours. It is in Him I trust, and it is in Him that I put my hope. Jesus is the One to make all things possible by trusting in You, by trusting in His blood that flows through me.

Behold my servant, whom I have chosen; my beloved, in whom my soul is well pleased: I will put my spirit upon him, and he shall shew judgment to the Gentiles. He shall not strive, nor cry; neither shall any man hear his voice in the streets. A bruised reed shall he not break, and smoking flax shall he not quench, till he send forth judgment unto victory. And in his name shall the Gentiles trust. (Matt. 12:18-21)

Your Thankful Servant

Letter 18

In the Secret Shelter

"Thou shalt hide them in the secret of thy presence from the pride of men:
thou shalt keep them secretly in a pavilion from the strife of tongues."
Psalm 31:20

Dear Jehovah,

God, You are my shelter, my secret shelter. In You, I am hidden with the presence of the Holy Spirit as my companion. From the enemy, I am secure in Your hiding place. To hide is to be concealed from something or someone. I can hide from myself, from love, from comfort, from anything. Most importantly, God, You hide me from the enemy within Your wings. Hiding from the enemy is wisdom, not cowardice. As the Scriptures say, "A prudent *man* foreseeth the evil, *and* hideth himself; *but* the simple pass on, *and* are punished" (Prov. 27:12).

This is not hiding of cowardice or fear; this is hiding of resting in Your presence and surrendering to You to fight my battles. You will open the eyes of the righteous and reveal the evil that surrounds them. Your eyes are always open to all evil. Even when Job was going through all his tragedies, he knew that, *"There is* no darkness, nor shadow of death, where the workers of iniquity may hide themselves" (Job 34:22). My enemy cannot run and hide from You, for You know all. Even if the enemy hides on top of a mountain, You will find him, and if he hides at the bottom of the ocean, You will surely find him. Lord, You bring judgment upon the enemy. You already have the victory, and I have the victory hidden in the presence of Your wings.

I am Your hidden one. Those that scheme against me will be destroyed by the fire of Jehovah. I am hidden in Your wings; You are my shelter where I will always find rest. And it is as, "He that dwelleth in the secret place of the most High shall abide under the shadow of the Almighty" (Ps. 91:1). Your presence is the essence of rest and peace that no one and no evil can conquer. You are my sword and my bow to fight against the evil amid Your wings. You, Lord, "Keep me as the apple of the eye, hide me under the shadow of thy wings" (Ps. 17:8).

Ever, Your presence is divine. Driven by the Holy Spirit, an indescribable experience. Eternal. The Holy Spirit is everywhere (see Ps. 139:7). Abba, You are protective (see Ps. 31:20) and joyful (Ps. 16:11), guiding (Exod. 33:14-15) Your children to their purpose for Your will, for Your glory (1 Chron. 16:27).

I *must* open my heart to Your presence and let You rule my heart. I want You to be my sanctuary, that you may dwell in me (see Exod. 25:8). Your presence is before me because of my Advocate, Jesus. He is what sets my tongue on fire, speaking Your heavenly language with the authority and power of Jesus. In Luke's account of the first Pentecost, I see how powerful the Holy Spirit is for those who fully accept You:

> And suddenly there came a sound from heaven as of a rushing mighty wind, and it filled all the house where they were sitting. And there appeared unto them cloven tongues like as of fire, and it sat upon each of them. And they were all filled with the Holy Ghost, and began to speak with other tongues, as

the Spirit gave them utterance. (Acts 2:2-4)

Jesus made this possible when He breathed His last breath. He became the Advocate for me in the presence of You, Father, by the Holy Spirit. Lord, Your presence is inviting. It is an invitation that I either accept or reject. There is not an in-between; it is either a yes or a no. Either my heart and soul are ready for Your presence or they are not. For Your presence is warmth, love, forgiveness, joy, protection, and . . . everlasting. Accepting Your presence is magnificent. I must accept Your presence every single day because You choose me every single day. I must seek You all the time. "One *thing* have I desired of the LORD, that will I seek after; that I may dwell in the house of the LORD all the days of my life, to behold the beauty of the LORD, and to inquire in his temple" (Ps. 27:4).

Dwelling in Your presence is a world in itself. Your presence is the heavenly kingdom I seek all the days of my life. As I abide in You, I will produce much fruit for the kingdom and glorify You. Jesus said, "I am the vine, ye *are* the branches: He that abideth in me, and I in him, the same bringeth forth much fruit: for without me ye can do nothing" (John 15:5).

Being covered by Your presence, God, is ethereal and eternal, but it also brings enemies—specifically, the enemy, Satan. The enemy knows whose Your people are just by Your presence and light that emanates from the soul. He knows that Your children have the authority and power to cast him down. He may know every weakness of mine, but He does not attack me because of my weaknesses. He attacks because of the strength that I have. He just uses my weaknesses against me. The strength I have is unbridled. It is a strength that is powerful and almighty with just an utterance, a strength that captures the victory with just one thought, cutting the enemy down. However, to wield Your strength, I must be humble. Alas, that is easier said than done.

Inevitably, I become prideful. It is a battle I face every day. The enemy takes advantage of that pride, but, God, You humble me before the throne. You let pride come before the downfall, ushering in humility before honor, bringing glory to You.

Pride is the enemy's feeble defense. In which that defense can be taken out with one swift punch. Though it can be taken and it may be a feeble defense, it does have a wicked punch that is vile, sinking its teeth into the heart and soul of humanity. The psalmist tells us about pride and its effects on those who fall prey to it:

> Pride compasseth them about as a chain; violence covereth them *as* a garment. Their eyes stand out with fatness: they have more than heart could wish. They are corrupt and speak wickedly *concerning* oppression: they speak loftily. They set their mouth against the heavens, and their tongue walketh through the earth. (Psalm 73:6-9)

The proud are violent (see Ps. 10), speak of sin (Ps. 59:12), oppress others (Ps. 94:3-7), and are haughty (Prov. 18:12). The proud make their thrones on a shaky and crumbling foundation. They claim Your position, but they are false gods with an abhorrent imagination.

Abba, in the Bible there are many people whose prideful hearts are ultimately crushed by Your hand. One of those people is the powerful man in the book of Esther named Haman. That story is about Esther becoming queen and saving her people, but it is also about the fall of Haman. As a high official of the king, even the king's officials had to bow down to him. But Haman was wicked, intending to destroy all Jews.

Aware of Haman's wickedness, Esther's relative Mordecai refused to bow before him. Haman took great offense at this. Mordecai was a Jew, and because of this, Haman took it upon himself to wipe out all the

Jews. Mordecai asked Esther to intervene to save her people. She did, thwarting Haman. But Haman was not done; He now wanted to kill Mordecai, but Esther's husband the king intervened, and Haman was the one who ended up being executed.

Lord, Haman abused his power because of his bruised pride. He became prideful when he became powerful, wanting to be on a pedestal above everyone else. Even above You, Jehovah. But God, You always prevail. You always have the victory. You are the power behind the power. Through the prophet Isaiah You have said,

> The lofty looks of man shall be humbled, and the haughtiness of men shall be bowed down, and the LORD alone shall be exalted in that day. For the day of the LORD of hosts *shall be* upon every *one that is* proud and lofty, and upon every *one that is* lifted up; and he shall be brought low. (Isa. 2:11-12)

The proud will always be brought to their knees before Your throne. A throne made of lies and a shaky foundation can never withstand Your throne. You will humble the boastful, and the boastful will fall. The psalmist says,

> Until I went into the sanctuary of God; *then* understood I their end. Surely thou didst set them in slippery places: thou castedst them down into destruction. How are they *brought* into desolation, as in a moment! they are utterly consumed with terrors. As a dream when *one* awakest; so, O Lord, when thou awakes, thou shalt despise their image. (Ps. 73:17-20)

The pride of humanity is everywhere, and it very damaging to people. Prideful people have a very sharp tongue and an unpredictable violent streak. People get hurt, and in response they sometimes act out or turn in upon themselves. Your people tend to gravitate to substitutes for You. However, what I must know is that You want all my hurt, anger, and bitterness. You want to mend and heal me. You want my surrender, for You are my protection and covering from the tongue of the prideful. Your Word and Your shadow are my covering as You told Isaiah, "I have put my words in thy mouth, and I have covered thee in the shadow of mine hand, that I may plant the heavens, and lay the foundations of the earth, and say unto Zion, Thou *art* my people" (Isa. 51:16). You cover me with the warmth of Your presence and with the strength of Your arms. Your coverings are healing, peace, forgiveness, and love. You are my protector, my rock, and my refuge. God, You are the secret shelter of my hurts, the secret shelter of my heart. I am at rest and at peace in the hidden shelter of You, Abba.

Abba, You have given us the ability to speak. The tongue can give life or death. It can be fruitful or fruitless. We communicate with our tongues. It is a delicate predicament. To speak is an expression of the character of the speaker. If one speaks life, then fruitfulness abounds. If one speaks death, then destruction will follow, with the sharp teeth of Satan crushing the fruit. A person's deathly speech is unreliable (see Ps. 5:9), deceitful (Ps. 120:2-3), boastful (Ps. 140:11), and rebellious (Prov. 10:31). It is like a lion's teeth that are sharp like spears and arrows, a tongue that cuts like a sword, slaying all prey within sight (Ps. 57:4). The tongue is wild, restless, and full of deadly poison. It cannot be tamed like a feral cat. Both blessing and cursing come from the tongue, which is perverse. Can a rose produce a lily? No, a rose can only produce a rose, and a lily can only produce a lily. Lord, that is the kind of power You have given us. Indeed, it is a very delicate predicament. We must be vigilant in what we speak, because

> every idle word that men shall speak, they shall give account thereof in the day of judgment. For by thy words thou shalt be

justified, and by thy words thou shalt be condemned. (Matt. 12:36-37)

On the other hand, the tongue is remarkable. You have blessed the tongue, so it can speak any language it chooses—love, forgiveness, promises, happiness, or joy. It can even be a gift from You, in the gift of prophecy, speaking in tongues, or interpretation. Yes, the tongue can even be a giver of life, but one must surrender their tongue to You, Lord. One must choose to be a giver of life, letting You clothe them in righteousness. For You said through Isaiah,

> Look unto me, and be ye saved, all the ends of the earth: for I *am* God, and *there is* non else. I have sworn by myself, the word is gone out of my mouth *in* righteousness, and shall not return, That unto me every knee shall bow, every tongue shall swear. (Isa. 45:22-23)

In righteousness, eyes, ears, and mouth are open to Your gloriousness. They are in tune with You, with Your will. A giver of life is the sustaining tongue, while the wicked tongue is a fracture in the spirit. King Solomon understood this when he wrote, "By long forbearing is a prince persuaded, and a soft tongue breaketh the bone" (Prov. 25:15). Yes, the giver of life speaks soothing, honey-dripped words that cut through the lies and hate. The words are like a thick, silver sword. Your people may be the light of the world, but they are warriors with voices that penetrates the heart of darkness, voices coated with steel that is unbreakable. Your voice is within, booming for all to hear. Abba, Your tongue will not be chained! Your people's tongues will not be chained. For You said, "So shall my word be that goeth forth out of my mouth: it shall not return unto me void, but it shall accomplish that which I please, and it shall prosper *in the thing* whereto I sent it" (Isa. 55:11).

Therefore, we speak forth life bringing fruitfulness to Your kingdom.

Your Humble Servant

Letter 19

Marvelous

"Blessed be the LORD: for he hath shewed me his marvellous kindness in a strong city."
Psalm 31:21

Dear Kindness,

Lips that speak life are lips that praise You, Lord. They glorify You. They worship You. They bless You. Usually, when I think of the word *bless*, I see You blessing me and Your people (such as I wake up every day or receiving Your healing and forgiveness). I do not see myself blessing You. It is true, though, that I can bless You by praising, glorifying, and worshipping You with all my heart and soul. By blessing You, You, in turn, bless me. Our relationship goes both ways. However, it is imperative for me to always, through the ups and downs, praise, worship, and glorify You. Praising You is expressing that You are most worthy. Praising You is why I am here; it is the very air I breathe. You enjoy those that constantly praise You; it is a symphony to Your ears. The psalmist rejoices and praises Your mighty name singing,

Rejoice in the LORD, O ye righteous: *for* praise is comely for the upright. Praise the LORD with harp: sing unto him with the psaltery *and* an instrument of ten strings. Sing unto him a new song; play skillfully with a loud noise. (Ps. 33:1-3)

Joy is upon Your heart when Your children praise Your glorious name. You do not care how or where I praise You. You only care that I do it with a sincere heart and soul. I can praise You in every form—in creation, in my history, in gratefulness, in forgiveness, and in love. When I praise You, my Abba, I don't praise You for myself, for that is conceited and most unworthy. Instead, my praise is only about You, Abba, and who You are. I must,

Give unto the LORD, O ye mighty, give unto the LORD glory and strength. Give unto the LORD the glory due unto his name; worship the LORD in the beauty of holiness. (Ps. 29:1-2)

Out of the loving praises for You come Your blessings.

A blessing is always from You. Your children are Your blessing. You made us in the image of Yourself, and You sacrificed Your Son for us. Your blessings are upon Your creation, and You bless Your creation through or by means of the creation. When You give Your blessings to Your creation, there are certain aspects that You *anticipate* from us. You test Your people with the tantalizing offer of Your divine promises. You must test our obedience, seeing if we can handle Your promises with spiritual maturity. We will not be alone in our trials, for You are always with us. You *want* us to come to You with all our trials. You *want* us to rely solely on You. Our survival is upon Your shoulders. For our sake, we *must* rely on You solely.

Our dependence on You is not without diligence. It is a race and an endurance test. We must never stop depending on You. We must depend on You at the mountaintop and depend on You in the valley. For, God, You reward those who seek only You, and it is a reward of a blessing. Our dependence means surrendering to You rather than declaring ourselves independent without need of You. A tottering choice must be made. Once that choice has been made, there is no looking back like Lot's wife. The choice is a finality with a blessing of beginnings.

God, You give Your blessings with an elegant grace otherwise unknown to humanity. Grace is Your love and favor that we truly do not deserve. Through Your grace, we are enabled to do Your good works, and through Your grace, we are saved by the incredible sacrifice of Jesus. Yes, "God *is* able to make all grace abound toward you; that ye, always having all sufficiency in all *things*, may abound to every good work" (2 Cor. 9:8). Your blessings are Your grace. Peter understood this by saying, "As every man hath received the gift, *even so* minister the same one to another, as good stewards of the manifold grace of God" (1 Pet. 4:10). Without Your grace, we would be desolate, but with Your grace, we can overcome anything. We can even overcome disobedience.

Disobedience is an ugly thorn. It is rebellion against You and brings forth Your wrath upon our neck. Disobedience is a sin that can only be washed by Your grace. You abhor disobedience, and You will certainly not give Your blessings to those who disobey You.

In Samuel's time, Saul had risen to become king, but he started to reject You who had made him king, looking to the self instead of to You. And Samuel rebuked Saul saying:

> Hath the LORD *as great* delight in burnt offerings and sacrifices, as in obeying the voice of the LORD? Behold, to obey *is* better than sacrifice, *and* to hearken than the fat of rams. For rebellion *is as* the sin of witchcraft, and stubbornness *is as* iniquity and idolatry. Because thou hast

rejected the word of the LORD, he hath also rejected thee from *being* king. (1 Sam. 15:22-23)

You will not give Your blessings to those who disobey Your Word, statutes, and commands. Ultimately, disobedience leads to missing out on Your blessings. Just as Deuteronomy teaches us, "The LORD shall make thee the head, and not the tail; thou shalt be above only, and thou shalt not be beneath; if that thou hearken unto the commandments of the LORD thy God, which I command thee this day, to observe and to do *them*" (28:13). With a fair warning, You give to us all. We mustn't test You or disobey You.

Turning our eyes upon You, we look with vigorous obedience. We look with a sparkle of marvel and loving-kindness at You who keep our hearts beating. For You are marvelous. You are being marvelous; it is an action, a verb that only You can perform. You are marvelous for all the blessings, miracles, and sacrifices You have given and endured for us, Your children. Lord, Your prophet Zechariah proclaimed, "If it be marvellous in the eyes of the remnant of this people in these days, should it also be marvellous in mine eyes? Saith the LORD of hosts" (Zech. 8:6). Marvelous is Your greatness. Marvelous is Your abundance, an abundance in faith we have that would shock Jesus off His feet. We must have a faith that believing the words Jesus spoke is enough to heal, forgive, love, and protect. We must have an abundant, outspoken faith that when "Jesus heard *it*, he marvelled" (Matt. 8:10).

God, You are loving-kindness, full of love, mercy, and goodness. Your kindness has three characteristics: strength, steadfastness, and love. You are our strength, our rock, our loyal and faithful God. And we must, "Know therefore that the LORD thy God, he *is* God, the faithful God, which keepeth covenant and mercy with them that love and keep his commandments for a thousand generations" (Deut. 7:9). Your kindness is extraordinary, acquired, developed, commended, and divine. These are ingredients not only of You, but of us too. Because You created us in Your image, we are what You are. Just as You are extraordinary, we are extraordinary. Just as You acquire our heart and soul, You challenge us to acquire all of You. "Put on therefore, as the elect of God, holy and beloved, bowels of mercies, kindness, humbleness of mind, meekness, longsuffering" (Col. 3:12). You develop Your kindness in our hearts as our relationship with You grows. It is a relationship that grows with praises of You on our lips and hearts. Knowing that You are our divine, eternal God, with a kindness that is of holiness.

Your Blessing Servant

Letter 20

Slow in Supplication

"For I said in my haste, I am cut off from before thine eyes: nevertheless thou heardest the voice of my supplications when I cried unto thee."
Psalm 31:22

Dear God of My Prayers,

Slow is a regressive word in society. Honestly, Lord, our inability to go slowly is a societal problem. Today speed and hastiness are promoted in the culture, while slowness is shunned. If I am too slow, there must be something wrong with me, but if I am hasty, striving for the next big thing, I am celebrated. When I watch people, I notice how fast everyone is going. People walk fast in the grocery store, order their food for fast delivery, or go from one place to the next so they can feel like they accomplished everything in one day. Sometimes I live like that. I live a hasty life. We live in a fast-paced world, a world that was built by human hands.

Ironically, being hasty can make me tremble with panic, a trembling that seizes my body so suddenly I feel I'm in peril. Hastiness leads to rash decisions that have severe consequences. This leads to the flesh taking over, throwing my spiritual life into disarray. It makes me unbalanced. Fear starts to creep in, quickly pushing You out of the way. Then comes the decision to rely upon myself as I watch my world crumble quickly and I become disobedient, bitter, and angry at You. But Your Word says, "*That* the soul *be* without knowledge, *it is* not good; and he that hasteth with *his* feet sinneth" (Prov. 19:2). Those that are hasty are foolish. I become foolish. I become self-made instead of God-made, quick to satisfy and obey the self with a prideful streak that corrupts the heart, vastly transforming the soul to reflect this black world.

But You, God, did not mold me to be fast-paced or hasty. You molded me to be slow and attentive to details. I am made to notice *all* Your creation, to take a deep breath, and to open my eyes to the slow-paced world You created for me. I look all around me and see that everything is growing in a progressive state. The flowers, the trees, the lull of the ocean, the gentle breeze, and . . . Your children. Even my relationship with You is slow. You do not just bless me with everything in one single moment. No, my relationship is nurtured by Your sculpting hands with setbacks and new growth and a love that is warm. Your slowness creates me to be all that I am supposed to be in Your image. I am slowly walking in Your purpose, taking sure and deliberate steps to fulfill all. Slowness opens the eyes, heart, ears, and soul to the colorfulness of Your Voice that knows me by my name. So I close my eyes, take a deep breath, and feel my heart beat the same slow rhythm as Yours. I feel Your connection to me. I feel Your slow pull for me to come nearer to You. Then I open my eyes and heart to the slowness of the world I was created for.

Lord, You have designated my eyes to seek and discern You, for You are the first to give the eyes the aptitude to see. And You do see me. I am the apple of Your eye. You will never lose sight of me. For "Behold, the eye of the LORD *is* upon them that fear him, upon them that hope in his mercy" (Ps. 33:18). You see all that takes place before Your kingdom and nations. You always know what is going on. You are *El Roi*, the God who sees. "Thine eyes did see my substance, yet being unperfect; and in thy book all *my members* were written, *which* in continuance were fashioned, when *as yet there was* none of them" (Ps. 139:16). Your eyes are honed with an apt judgment of Your creation. Your eyes are ever-present upon the nations that You have created, and You let no defiance rise against Yourself. For You will strike down any who rebel against You. Just as the psalmists explains,

> He that planted the ear, shall he not hear? he that formed the eye, shall he not see? He that chastiseth the heathen, shall not he correct? he that teacheth man knowledge, shall not he know? The LORD knoweth the thoughts of man, that they are vanity. (Ps. 94:9-11)

Those who are judged unjustly are judged rightly by You, God Almighty. Though You judge us rightly, You are also our seeing protector, our truth seeker. You watch over those who are righteous, those who do right, and You hear their prayers. But those who do evil You turn Your eyes away from. You see the truth of who they are. When the righteous pray, they pray earnestly to You as Jeremiah did: "O LORD, *are* not thine eyes upon the truth? thou hast stricken them, but they have not grieved; thou hast consumed them, *but* they have refused to receive correction: they have made their faces harder than a rock; they have refused to return" (Jer. 5:3). You are seer of all things.

You are a seer who hears our supplications and our prayers. When we pray, it is a request to You, an outpouring of the heart, and a deeper connection. It is a pleasing aroma. Every time we pray, *You hear* but You always hear with a purpose. You hear our pleas and cries. Your ear is of our heart and mind. With an attentive true ear, You understand the prayers of Your children. With that attentiveness, we know whose we belong to. We have a God whom we have called upon, "for thou wilt hear me, O God: incline thine ear unto me, *and hear* my speech" (Ps. 17:6). Those who are for Your will and are righteous according to Your will, You hear them. You hear me. With great assurance I know, "This is the confidence that we have in him, that, if we ask any thing according to his will, he heareth us" (1 John 5:14). Most unfortunately, those who are against Your purpose and whose hearts are hardened You turn Your ears away, "but if any man be a worshipper of God, and doeth his will, him he heareth" (John 9:31). But oh yes, Your ear is not "heavy, that it cannot hear" (Isa. 59:1)!

You are the One to open our ears to hear Your Word. Little by little, new day after new day, You open my eyes and ears to understanding Your will and purposes. But it is my job to accept and obey Your Voice with discernment. "Verily, verily, I say unto you, He that heareth my word, and believeth on him that sent me, hath everlasting life, and shall not come into condemnation; but is passed from death unto life" (John 5:24). Without discernment, then, my flesh and the enemy will be the decision-makers and my ears will be tone deaf. Yet discernment is within me. I just need to let the Holy Spirit guide me and to hear Your sweet Voice guide my feet.

Prayer is relational. It is a relationship between You and myself. You will only take as much as I give. It is a conversation with You, not a demand; you do not take from me. A conversation with You is like a gentle push and pull from the waves of the ocean. Yes, prayer is essential to being intimate with You, more connected with You. You value every time I pray to You. You love it when I pray, because then You can answer me, heal me, forgive me, bring peace to me, and do Your will through me. As I pray to You, an overwhelming sense of confidence surges through my being. It is a confidence that comes from being obedient to You, because surely, praying is an act of obedience. Though You give peace, confidence, and love during prayer, I must be humble before

You. I must give all my heart and soul to You, for You are the One who created me. You hear every word, every whisper, and every tear. In times of trouble, You hear, but I must go to prayer first. Even when You have blessed me, I must go to prayer to give You thanks and glory. I trust You. You are there and You hear. At rest I am. I close my eyes, hear You breathe, and listen to Your Voice. I tune everything out but You. I recite this verse, "Thine ears shall hear a word behind thee, saying, This *is* the way, walk ye in it, when ye turn to the right hand, and when ye turn to the left" (Isa. 30:21).

Sometimes my prayers do not get answered the way I want them to. Sometimes they do. But *always* my prayers are answered by Your will. You have my best interests at heart. I am the apple of Your eye. I must have patience. With the psalmist I say, "I waited patiently for the LORD; and he inclined unto me, and heard my cry" (Ps. 40:1). I must never feel discouraged if my prayer has not been fulfilled, because You have something much better for me than what I want. You have what I desperately *need*. I cannot lose faith in an unanswered prayer because right behind my unanswered prayer is my victory.

I must first be cleansed every day. I must believe, speak my prayers with confidence in Jesus's name, and I must always keep my prayers aligned with Your will. I sin every single day. Some may be minor sins or major sins, but in the end, they are all sins. Sins that hurt You. Sins that hurt Jesus. He died for me so I could be cleansed, but I must decide. The decision comes down to dropping to my knees, seeking Your face, and asking You to forgive me of all my sins, to cleanse me of them, to be washed with the blood of Jesus Christ. Then again, to be cleansed I must believe that You, God, exist, that You can cleanse me of all sins no matter how egregious, that the impossible is made possible. I must believe in the prayers that come forth from the lips. Believe that my prayers were answered and they will come to fruition.

As Jesus says,

Verily I say unto you, If ye have faith, and doubt not, ye shall not only do this *which is done* to the fig tree, but also if ye shall say unto this mountain, Be thou removed, and be thou cast into the sea; it shall be done. And all things, whatsoever ye shall ask in prayer, believing, ye shall receive. (Matt. 21:21-22).

All of this is done in Jesus's name. His name is powerful. It is so powerful that the enemy's knees shake with fear. With just a whisper—no, with just a thought of His name—I already have the victory. I have Your ear.

And whatsoever ye shall ask in my name, that will I do, that the Father may be glorified in the Son. If ye shall ask any thing in my name, I will do *it*. (John 14:13-14)

My prayers must coincide with Your will. Not my will, Your will. Your purposes. My will is inferior to Your will. I only know a fraction of Your wisdom, knowledge, and purposes. It is You who reveal fragment by fragment. If I knew all Your will, then most likely I would run away from Your purpose. Or my pride and selfishness would get in the way of Your will. I must always set aside my purpose and put forth Yours in my prayers. For "This is the confidence that we have in him, that, if we ask anything according to his will, he heareth us" (1 John 5:14).

Prayer is my need. It brings me closer to You, melding the chords of the relationship into an unbreakable bond. It is glorifying You, praising You, and worshipping You. It is adoration of the One who has never abandoned me in the dark and a confession of my deepest heart. Prayer is the healing balm of my heart and the connector of my heartstrings. It is the weapon of my warfare in the spiritual battle and the shield of protection. Yes, prayer is my authoritative and all-powerful arsenal. I must not misuse it, for You will surely not hear me. Instead, I must bring You the honor and glory of using my voice for Your will.

Your Praying Servant

Letter 21

Faithful Perseverance

"O love the LORD, all ye his saints: for the LORD preserveth the faithful,
and plentifully rewardeth the proud doer."
Psalm 31:23

Dear God,

You are love. Love is You. An everlasting binding-love. A fulfilling warmth blanketed with conviction in my heart. You are many things, but Your love truly conquers all. A holy love. Without Your love, I would be doomed. You would strike me down the instant I sinned. I would know no mercy or grace, and Jesus would not have died on the cross for me. I would not love others. Everything You do for me comes from deep, unfathomable love. You show me Your forgiving love so that I may love others. You heal with love, convict with love, protect, provide, sanctify, and make my heart beat with love. I am Your first love. It is so amazing to know the kind of God I have, the kind of God that beckons on my behalf. You are known by many things and many names: Yahweh, Jehovah, Elohim. There can never be enough names for You, my Lord, but simply *Abba* is enough. Abba, You are my Father, so full of love. You command presence with gentleness and convict with fatherly love.

Your love is for everyone, but Your love transcends through the godly, the saints. You pour upon Your people a heart-gripping and fulfilling love that is beyond our worldly comprehension. The godly are guided by Your grace to live according to whose they are, not self-made or altered by the world but made by the living God. Made in Your image. Transformed by Your might and love. Forgive me, Lord, if I have made Your people seem less godly. That was not my intention. The godly are Your people who seek You with all their heart and soul. The godly know in whom their identity is found. The godly are filled with the presence of the Holy Spirit, opening their eyes, ears, heart, and soul to who You are, discerning what is good and evil, and what Your will is.

However, there is a duty that must be done on Your people's behalf, and that duty is holiness. Paul writes of You choosing us to be holy, "He hath chosen us in him before the foundation of the world, that we should be holy and without blame before him in love" (Eph. 1:4). Holiness is Your foundation for the godly. It is our foundation to stay godly, being sanctified in Your holiness. A holy foundation is a faithful foundation. Without faith there is no foundation; there is no You, God. "But without faith *it is* impossible to please *him*: for he that cometh to God must believe that he is, and that he is a rewarder of them that diligently seek him" (Heb. 11:6). A faith of holiness is flowing with love, the love of Christ. Your love brings patience and kindness. It does not become jealous or prideful. It knows no record of being wronged, and there is no joy in injustice. This love, this love is holy, never loses faith, is hopeful, and endures through every circumstance. The godly are to be this love. Your people are to be godly.

Those who love You and choose to be godly are those who You preserve. To preserve, according to Strong's Concordance, means "to watch, to guard, to keep." The Hebrew word is *natsar*. Thus, You are watching, guarding, and keeping the faithful at the palm of Your hand. I cannot stress enough that we must *believe* in You who are faithful to us, for You are our deliverer and our refuge from enemies. You are the God who speaks assuredly and clearly. There is no other who commands with such power that the godly have no other choice but to obey the Voice. Yes! Believing in You, God Almighty is believing that You do watch, guard, and keep us from our enemies. Lord, the words of the psalmist reverberate inside my soul: "Because he hath set his love upon me, therefore will I deliver him: I will set him on high, because he hath known by my name" (Ps. 91:14).

You rescue those who love You, and You are faithful to those who trust in Your name. Ever the Protector, You hide the faithful in the shadow of Your wings. We will not cower or become fearful or distraught by what we see in front of us, all around us. We must not look at our dismal circumstances. Instead, we close our eyes, feel our heartbeat, hear Your breath, God, and see the cross. We surrender to the Holy Spirit and let You work within our heart and soul. You heal us, cleanse us, and open our eyes to Your goodness amid our circumstances. You are always there, ever faithful to us, even when at times it may not seem so. We must open our eyes to how You preserve us from the enemy.

Consequently, You preserving us hangs on the precipice of our faith. Our faith must endure through the wreckage of our ship. We must stand fast to the true belief of our origin. You are our origin. Our identity is made known to us by Your image, the One we place our faith in, not in ourselves but in You who are first faithful to us. What You have done is Your faithfulness, and what You will do is Your trustworthiness. It is by Your grace and mercy that we receive Your faithfulness every day. You do not have to prove Yourself to us. We do not demand it from You. By keeping Your covenants to Your children, You have already proven Yourself. Your action of faithfulness is an act of fully trusting in us. The same goes for Your people. Even just considering something to be trustworthy is an act of fully believing in it. Having faith in You involves a choice. We choose to yearn for a deeper personal relationship with You. We come to understand Your ways, Your love, Your forgiveness, and Your presence. Being faithful to You is having a loyal heart. Loyalty is, without a doubt, an enduring commitment. I may seem to exaggerate, but if I am not willing to die for You, my Father, then am I really putting You first above all else? Jesus died on the cross. For me. Do I love You as much as You do me? That is the kind of loyalty I want to have.

> Who shall separate us from the love of Christ? *shall* tribulation, or distress, or persecution, or famine, or nakedness, or peril, or sword? As it is written, For thy sake we are killed all the day long; we are accounted as sheep for the slaughter. Nay, in all these things we are more than conquerors through him that loved us. (Rom. 8:35-37)

Just as You are loyal to us, we must reciprocate that same loyalty. It is what You desire. It is a pleasing aroma to You. Our loyalty to You fuels our faith in You, a faith that is an everlasting shield against the prideful. You lift the faithful and knock down the prideful.

Turning from faithful to prideful will surely be our downfall. Faith and pride are very delicate issues. With faith, we must constantly put ourselves last and put You, Lord, first. However, with pride, it is the opposite. Pride destroys the budding flower. It wrecks one's perseverance of faith. Though pride is arrogance, conceit, and haughtiness at the core, it is more simply uncertainty. It is uncertainty that You will do as You have said You will do, uncertainty that our faith in You is strong enough to endure. Thus, we turn away from our Creator and we turn toward ourselves. We rely only on *ourselves*, because *we* think *we* can accomplish it, whatever *it* is.

Pride craves a platform. Abba, pride craves our hearts. It wants to infect our hearts with insecurities, doubt, uncertainty, and forgetfulness of whose we are. As the prophet Ezekiel said to the prince of Tyrus, "Because thine heart *is* lifted up, and thou hast said, I *am* a God, I sit *in* the seat of God, in the midst of the seas; yet thou *art* a man, and not God, though thou set thine heart as the heart of God" (Ezek. 28:2). Every day we must get down on our knees and ask You to humble our hearts. We must be sincere in our humility because You do not like proud people. We must not become like Pharaoh or Haman in Esther or even the disciples. We always stay alert to our heart, always be humble in whose we are.

Your Persevering Servant

Letter 22

Courage

"Be of good courage, and he shall strengthen your heart, all ye that hope in the LORD."
Psalm 31:24

Dear Courage,

As I begin this last letter, Lord I pray to Your people that their heart is fully opened to You, heading Your warnings, and having been transformed by the Holy Spirit. God, I leave with them the hope, love, and strength of You.

Jehovah, *courage* is an interesting word. Others will tell colleagues, friends, or family to have courage in the face of trials, but they do not put that same word into action themselves. It is a word that is easier said than done. Many times, Lord, in my walk with You, in my trials, I have come face to face with the words *courage* and *cowardice*. When it gets tough, do I choose courage over cowardice or cowardice over courage? Yes, I make that mistake of choosing to fear as we all do, but the real question is what do I do with the aftermath? Give up? Turn my back on You? Label myself as worthless?

No, I cannot do any of that! I cannot just give up after one cowardly mistake! I cannot be the face of Your anger God. You will not destroy me. You could only love me. Granted, there will be a reprimand, because You are my Father. But You will not forsake me. You forgive, You love, You protect, You encourage. Just as what You spoke to the Israelites, You speak to me, to my heart: "Be strong and of a good courage, fear not, nor be afraid of them: for the LORD thy God, he *it is* that doth go with thee; he will not fail thee, nor forsake thee" (Deut. 31:6).

Courage is a very delicate, graceful strength. It is strength of heart. You communicate courage to Your people. You seek courage-filled hearts. Your Scriptures say, "The eyes of the LORD run to and fro throughout the whole earth, to shew himself strong in the behalf of *them* whose heart *is* perfect toward him" (2 Chron. 16:9). I must have an expectancy of victory, God, Your victory, and Your will toward Your purposes for me and the world. I cannot be walking on thin ice; I must have confidence, a belief that Your power is sufficient in my weaknesses. I have to have an expectancy of courage to walk on that thin ice. Even when the ice breaks, my heart of courage walks on water with the right hand of Jesus. I must never waiver in that courage of belief.

Courage brings strength of the heart, a strong beat and a steady pulse. First and foremost, strength only comes from You. No amount of physical strength will yield Your fruits. This strength that is of courage is purely eternal, spiritual, and holy. It is in my innermost being, my soul and my heart. I can see this strength in all Your creation. My eyes constantly need to be opened to see Your marvelousness. I see it in the fall of rain that can bring forth beautiful flowers or in the deep blue unknown ocean that has magnificent mysteries. But to see in Your strength that is holy, is to find the tiny mustard seed of faith or the lilies of rebirth. To see at night the stars of beauty that gazes back with an ethereal purity. For to "Lift up your eyes on high, and behold who hath created these *things*, that bringeth out their host by number: he calleth them all by names by the greatness of his might, for that *he is* strong in power; not one faileth" (Isa. 40:26).

Yet, out of all creation, You chose to put Your strength in me, to do Your will and purposes. Your strength in me opens my eyes to Your eternity, your spiritual world, and your holiness within me. You *chose* me. I have the strength of Jesus! For His blood, the blood that fell at the cross, courses through my veins. The strength is within me. Hallelujah! I glorify You! Praise You, God! I speak forth Your name with the strength of Your blood on my lips! It is the strength of Jesus, "who being the brightness of *his* glory, and the express image of his person, and upholding all things by the word of his power, when he had by himself purged our sins, sat down on the right hand of the Majesty on high" (Heb. 1:3).

To be strong *is* to cry, to *be* vulnerable, to *call out* my weaknesses, and to *humble* myself before *El Roi*, the God who sees me. Using my own strength brings destruction, destruction to my heart and soul, destruction to me or the ones I love. But to forfeit my strength and to surrender to You, Lord, to use all Your strength, is to be strong indeed. Even to love You with everything I have is to be strong, for it takes a strong person to lay down all their vulnerabilities, all their weaknesses at the cross, to be wrenched open with all their bleeding wounds and to lay herself in the palm of Your hand. It is You I rely on to give me the strength to get back up and praise You, to be strong in the courage You have blessed me with. Yes "Both riches and honour *come* of thee, and thou reignest over all; and in thine hand *is* power and might; and in thine hand *it is* to make great, and to give strength unto all" (1 Chron. 29:12).

Courage is strength and the heart is strength. I must first have my heart right before Your courage and strength can take root. My heart must echo what the soul is. For my heart deceives and is the seat of my emotions. The emotions of love, forgiveness, kindness, hate, anger, or bitterness can be the drivers of my heart. Most of my emotions are derived from my personality. My personality is what makes me unique, makes me stand out from everyone else. This can be a good thing, but it can also be wrought by pride. Thus, Jehovah, You look at the heart, not my actions. My heart can be one of evil yet, my actions say otherwise. In 1 Samuel 16, God, You sent Samuel to Bethlehem to find the next king of Israel. The family that Samuel was sent to had many sons. When Samuel saw one of the sons, for His appearance was one of great physical strength, he announced that surely God had anointed him. But You responded to Samuel, "Look not on his countenance, or on the height of his stature; because I have refused him: for *the LORD seeth* not as man seeth; for man looketh on the outward appearance, but the LORD looketh on the heart" (1 Sam. 16:7). The next sons came forward and Samuel rejected them, but there was one more son, who'd been attending his flock when his brothers were being introduced. This son didn't have the same physical stature as his brothers. However, Samuel asked for him to come forth and with his spiritual eyes open, the Lord revealed to him that he was to be the king of Israel. That son, that shepherd boy, was David.

My heart determines my faithfulness to You. For everything flows from the heart—trust, faith, love, doubt, or insecurity. The path I choose determines the fragility of my heart. Even though in my mind I think I have chosen the path first, my heart speaks otherwise. For the heart is a function of the mind. It is the one to first choose a course of action. That is why You look in the heart rather than the mind. You tell us through the prophet Jeremiah, "I the LORD search the heart, *I* try the reins, even to give every man according to his ways, *and* according to the fruit of his doings" (Jer. 17:10). You are the examiner, the judge. Moreover, You are also my heart, because You are my Creator. I am Your image; thus, my heart *is* Your heart. You are the One to take away the stubbornness of my heart and to give me a new heart, a new spirit within. You are the Breath of Life.

Courage with the strength of the heart is only grasped with hope in You. Hope is the expectation of what is to come. It is expecting Your goodness. This hope is not just found randomly; it is found by knowing You and what You have already done for me. Your character and what You have done in the past are the foundation for my hope in the future. By Your Word, my hope is placed in. Your Word describes who You are, Your character. But what solidifies my hope is my experience of You. My experience of Your fulfillment of promises, Your love, Your kindness, Your forgiveness, Your grace, and Your mercy. When I see, hear, and feel You in my life, my hope grows. It seeks more of You, more of Your promises, more of Your will, and more of Your purposes.

My hope will be stretched thin and sometimes it will feel like I cannot possibly go on. I cannot hope for more. However, I must not give in to the temptation of defeat and despair. That is exactly what the enemy wants. He wants to snatch my hope away. Without hope, I will not believe that You will do what You have promised to do. I will not believe what I *can* do. Thus, hope is about eagerly waiting with patience that is clothed in Your steadfast love and unshakable courage, bringing joy, faith, perseverance, and endurance. As Paul wrote to the Christians of Rome,

And not only *so*, but we glory in tribulations also: knowing that tribulation worketh patience; and patience, experience; and experience, hope: And hope maketh not ashamed; because the love of God is shed abroad in our hearts by the Holy Ghost which is given unto us." (Rom. 5:3-5)

Hope is Jesus Christ. You are the One that hope originates from. The Good News that Jesus spoke of, prophesied, and demonstrated is filled with hope for the eternal, an eternal reserved only for Your people. I must expect what You have for me. I must expect what Jesus died on the cross for.

Therefore being justified by faith, we have peace with God through our Lord Jesus Christ: By whom also we have access by faith into this grace wherein we stand, and rejoice in hope of the glory of God. (Rom. 5:1-2)

I look within my heart, a heart that only blossoms with everlasting hope from Jesus. My heart is watered by the blood of Jesus Christ. With assurances I have the hope to, "hold fast the profession of *our* faith without wavering; (for he *is* faithful that promised)" (Heb. 10:23).

Your Courageous Servant

Notes

Letter 1

1. Leland Ryken et al., *Dictionary of Biblical Imagery,* (Downers Grove, Illinois: InterVarsity Press, 1998) 262.

2. Ryken et al., *Dictionary of Biblical Imagery*, 261

Letter 2

3.Ryken et al., *Dictionary of Biblical Imagery*, 732

Letter 4

4.Ryken et al., *Dictionary of Biblical Imagery*, 885

Letter 17

5.Ryken et al., *Dictionary of Biblical Imagery*, 343-344

Resources

Ryken, Leland, James C. Wilhoit, and Tremper Longman, eds. *Dictionary of Biblical Imagery*. Downers Grove, Illinois: InterVarsity Press, 1998.

Strong, James. *The New Strong's Expanded Exhaustive Concordance of the Bible*. Nashville: Thomas Nelson, 2010.

About the Author

Kaela Saner can usually be found cozied up in a blanket reading a book and studying the Bible. Her passion is God and she is constantly learning something new from Him. Writing I Trust You, Lord: Letters to God on Psalm 31, is her way of expressing God's character to His people. When not absorbed in the Bible or writing, Kaela loves being with her family, coaching basketball, and being outdoors. She lives in Florence, KY with her family.

Made in the USA
Columbia, SC
09 July 2021

41609763R00070